AMERICAN ★ HISTORY

BATTLING TERRORISM
in the United States

By Caroline Kennon

Published in 2018 by
Lucent Press, an Imprint of Greenhaven Publishing, LLC
353 3rd Avenue
Suite 255
New York, NY 10010

Copyright © 2018 Lucent Press, an Imprint of Greenhaven Publishing, LLC.

All rights reserved. No part of this book may be reproduced in any form without permission in writing from the publisher, except by a reviewer.

Designer: Deanna Paternostro
Editor: Siyavush Saidian

Library of Congress Cataloging-in-Publication Data

Names: Kennon, Caroline.
Title: Battling terrorism in the United States / Caroline Kennon.
Description: New York : Lucent Press, 2018. | Series: American history | Includes index.
Identifiers: ISBN 9781534561410 (library bound) | ISBN 9781534561427 (ebook)
Subjects: LCSH: Terrorism–Juvenile literature. | Terrorism–Prevention–Juvenile literature.
Classification: LCC HV6431.K425 2018 | DDC 303.6–dc23

Printed in the United States of America

CPSIA compliance information: Batch #BS17KL: For further information contact Greenhaven Publishing LLC, New York, New York at 1-844-317-7404.

Please visit our website, www.greenhavenpublishing.com. For a free color catalog of all our high-quality books, call toll free 1-844-317-7404 or fax 1-844-317-7405.

Contents

Foreword	4
Setting the Scene: A Timeline	6
Introduction:	
What Is Terrorism?	8
Chapter One:	
Terrorism in 19th Century America	12
Chapter Two:	
Terrorism in 20th Century America	23
Chapter Three:	
Domestic Bombings	36
Chapter Four:	
Al-Qaeda and the World Trade Center Attacks	56
Chapter Five:	
Terrorism After September 11	70
Epilogue:	
Battling Terrorism Today	82
Notes	93
For More Information	97
Index	99
Picture Credits	103
About the Author	104

Foreword

The United States is a relatively young country. It has existed as its own nation for more than 200 years, but compared to nations such as China that have existed since ancient times, it is still in its infancy. However, the United States has grown and accomplished much since its birth in 1776. What started as a loose confederation of former British colonies has grown into a major world power whose influence is felt around the globe.

How did the United States manage to develop into a global superpower in such a short time? The answer lies in a close study of its unique history. The story of America is unlike any other—filled with colorful characters, a variety of exciting settings, and events too incredible to be anything other than true.

Too often, the experience of history is lost among the basic facts: names, dates, places, laws, treaties, and battles. These fill countless textbooks, but they are rarely compelling on their own. Far more interesting are the stories that surround those

basic facts. It is in discovering those stories that students are able to see history as a subject filled with life—and a subject that says as much about the present as it does about the past.

The titles in this series allow readers to immerse themselves in the action at pivotal historical moments. They also encourage readers to discuss complex issues in American history—many of which still affect Americans today. These include racism, states' rights, civil liberties, and many other topics that are in the news today but have their roots in the earliest days of America. As such, readers are encouraged to think critically about history and current events.

Each title is filled with excellent tools for research and analysis. Fully cited quotations from historical figures, letters, speeches, and documents provide students with firsthand accounts of major events. Primary sources bring authority to the text, as well. Sidebars highlight these quotes and primary sources, as well as interesting figures and events. Annotated bibliographies allow students to locate and evaluate sources for further information on the subject.

A deep understanding of America's past is necessary to understand its present and its future. Sometimes you have to look back to see how to best move forward, and that is certainly true when writing the next chapter in the American story.

Setting the Scene:

1857
The Mountain Meadows Massacre is the first major account of terrorism documented in American history.

1963
A dynamite explosion, caused by the Ku Klux Klan (KKK), kills four girls at the 16th Street Baptist Church in Birmingham, Alabama.

1986
The CIA establishes the Counterterrorism Center (CTC) as a division of the National Clandestine Service.

1857   1873   1947–1952   1963   1978   1986   1993

1873
Dozens of black people and Radical Republicans are killed by white supremacists in the Colfax Massacre.

1978
Ted Kaczynski (the Unabomber) sends his first bomb to a University of Illinois professor of rocket science.

1947–1952
The Central Intelligence Agency (CIA) and National Security Agency (NSA) are formed.

1993
Ramzi Yousef and 6 other Muslim extremists detonate a bomb beneath the World Trade Center in New York, killing 6 and injuring more than 1,000; the United States learns of Osama bin Laden when his phone number is among the list of calls made by Yousef after the terrorist attack.

Battling Terrorism in the United States

A Timeline

1995–1998
Timothy McVeigh bombs a federal building in Oklahoma City, killing 168 and injuring more than 500; the Unabomber is found after killing 3 and seriously injuring 2 with 16 bombings; Osama bin Laden issues the Declaration of Jihad on the Americans Occupying the Country of the Two Holiest Sites, intending to start a war with the United States.

2016
Omar Mateen opens fire in an Orlando, Florida, nightclub, killing 49 people and injuring 53 in the worst mass shooting in U.S. history.

| 1995–1998 | 2001 | 2009–2011 | 2013 | 2014–2015 | 2016 |

2001
Jihadists hijack four planes and crash them into the World Trade Center in New York, the Pentagon outside Washington, D.C., and a field in Pennsylvania, killing nearly 3,000 people; President George W. Bush declares a war on terror.

2009–2011
Major Nidal Malik Hasan kills 13 people and injures 32 in a mass shooting at the Fort Hood military base; Navy SEALs secretly fly into Pakistan and kill bin Laden.

2013
Two bombs go off near the finish line of the Boston Marathon, killing three people; the Islamic State of Iraq and Syria (ISIS) is founded by Abu Bakr al-Baghdadi.

2014–2015
Ivan Lopez kills three people and injures 16 before killing himself at Fort Hood; Mohammad Youssuf Abdulazeez shoots 7 people and kills 5 at the Navy Operations Support Center in Chattanooga; Syed Rizwan Farook and Tashfeen Malik open fire at a holiday party in San Bernardino, killing 14 people and injuring 21.

Introduction

WHAT IS TERRORISM?

One of the most common terms in modern day media is "terrorism." People around the world are familiar with it and the feeling of fear it strikes in people. As of the 21st century, terrorism has become strongly associated with groups similar to the Islamic State of Iraq and Syria, or ISIS, and attacks such as those that occurred on September 11, 2001. However, terrorism has existed for centuries; it can be found throughout world history and within every era of American history. Terrorism can be used to describe any number of violent acts committed by any kind of person or people.

The Federal Bureau of Investigation (FBI) and other law enforcement agencies insist there is no single, correct way to describe terrorism, but the U.S. federal code defines it as "the unlawful use of force and violence against persons or property to intimidate or coerce a government, the civilian population, or any segment thereof, in furtherance of political or social objectives."[1] This means that crimes committed between two individuals motivated by personal feelings would not qualify as terrorism, but if one person commits a violent crime against a larger group with the intent to frighten them, that could be defined as terrorism.

The Rise of Terrorism

Ever since the dawn of the 21st century, humanity has been living in the most terrorist-aware time in history. The rise of instant communication and digital media has allowed information on terrorist attacks to spread around the world at an unprecedented pace. Terrorists have used this media coverage to their advantage by expanding attacks. In 2016, 86 people were killed on a beach in Nice, France; a Catholic priest was murdered in a church in Normandy, France;

Year	Western Europe Approximate Deaths	United States Approximate Deaths
1972	300	10
1980	300	10
1988	300	5
1995	50	150
2001	50	3000
2004	150	0
2015	150	50

This table, adapted from information published in Economist, *shows a comparison between European and American deaths from terrorist actions.*

and 12 people were killed at a Christmas Market in Berlin, Germany—all in the name of terrorism. A mass shooting at an Orlando, Florida, nightclub in June 2016 worsened the fear that most Americans have about terrorist attacks.

September 11, 2001, was a tragic day. Since then, security and intelligence have been successful in preventing many international terrorist plots from reaching domestic soil. Airlines now take maximum precautions with the screening of passengers, federal agents can spot potential terrorist plots, and local police are trained to better protect their citizens. Despite these advancements in security, terrorism continues to claim lives. Targets are often chosen for their cultural symbolism to make a large and deliberate statement. Some attacks have involved trained terrorists from the Middle East, but most domestic terrorist attacks have been the work of American citizens who sympathize with terrorism groups and have never been to Syria, Iraq, or Afghanistan. This threat is more difficult to combat than an airplane hijacking, since anyone can find a truck and drive it into a crowd, potentially killing dozens. In the United States, it is also relatively easy to buy guns, which can be used for mass shootings.

Taking Chances

Although the number of terrorist-related deaths in the 1970s in Europe were high, the chance of being killed was small. In the 30 years of the Northern Ireland Troubles, the annual risk of being killed in Ulster, Northern Ireland, was 1 in 25,000. In the United States in the 21st century, that number is even lower: The risk of an American being killed in a terrorist attack in 2001 was less than

1 in 100,000. Between 2001 and 2013, the chance was 1 in 56 million. The chance of being killed in a homicide in the United States is roughly 1 in 20,000. Car accidents are about twice as likely to result in death as a violent crime.

On average, North America experiences fewer terrorist attacks than other regions. Western Europe gets hit frequently, but South Asia, the Middle East, and North Africa have the most reported instances of terrorism. The point of terrorism is to make people afraid, but the odds of any given individual being killed in an attack are actually low. A series of major terrorist attacks in Paris, France, in 2015 killed about 130, but about three times that number of French people died that same day from cancer. The attacks on the United States on September 11 were catastrophic, but it is more likely for the average American to be crushed to death by unstable furniture than die from a terrorist attack. Daniel Kahneman, a professor at Princeton University, stated that even "in countries that have been targets of intensive terror campaigns, such as Israel, the weekly number of casualties almost never [comes] close to the number of traffic deaths."[2]

The Terror of Terrorism

Why, then, are millions of people afraid of terrorism, even though the odds of an attack are so low? People often dread what they feel they cannot control, and terrorism can harm a large amount of people at once. After September 11, many were afraid to fly, so they drove to their destinations instead. Ironically, experts calculated that more people died from the resulting car accidents than the number of those killed on the four planes hijacked by al-Qaeda. Cars are more dangerous than planes, but in a car, individuals feel they have more control. The odds of dying in a terrorist attack in the United States are significantly lower than dying due to an everyday action, such as driving, or due to drug overdoses or gun violence. That does not, however, mean that terrorism is not a significant threat.

Terrorists employ psychological warfare against whatever society they are trying to intimidate and scare. The emotional effects of terrorism are always much greater than the actual lethality of the attack, and both are important aspects of terrorist attacks. This is partially due to the intense and immediate media coverage that attacks receive, as well as the way politicians react and the obviously increased presence of additional security. Terrorism frightens more than most other traumatic and violent events, affecting even those nowhere near the location of the attacks, because of how random the attacks seem and how anyone could be an attacker. Despite the increase in Islamophobia—a prejudicial and often racist fear of Muslims and Middle Easterners because some prominent terror groups are from that geographical area—in the 2010s, terrorism itself is not a concept unique to the Middle East. Moreover, it is not even new in U.S. history.

It is undeniable that the United States has a past that includes instances of domestic terror. It is not a new or recent phenomenon, and how the United States has identified and battled terror throughout the centuries has changed greatly as terrorism itself has evolved. Why some are motivated to aggressively attack others and commit acts of violence—while most others do not—is a question that might not ever be answered. Not much is understood about the psychology of a terrorist. Sometimes, terrorists are born in poverty or isolation, whether physical or emotional. Some Muslim terrorists, such as members of ISIS and al-Qaeda, believe the violent acts are pleasing to the teachings of Islam and Allah—even though Islam does not teach this. Some terrorists throughout history have suffered from mental illness, and others have been well-educated and intelligent. Regardless, most terrorists have the intent to negatively influence a specific population, and a major aspect of this is taking responsibility for the violence so that this population knows exactly who to be terrified of.

Chapter One

TERRORISM IN 19TH CENTURY AMERICA

Before the founding of the United States in the 18th century, there were most likely no official instances of terrorism in the 13 colonies. However, from the perspective of the colonies' rulers in England, the Continental Army probably seemed like a terrorist group. The English most likely viewed revolutionary incidents, such as the Boston Tea Party, as forms of terrorism. However, the American Revolution was not trying to intimidate the colonial lords—its soldiers simply fought for independence.

After the war, the new American government capitalized on the national spirit of goodwill and excitement for a new era of prosperity. As such, there were no recorded instances of what modern-day scholars define as domestic terrorism for decades after the revolution. It was not until the mid-19th century that this changed with the Mountain Meadows Massacre.

Mountain Meadows Massacre

The first major account of terrorism documented in American history is the Mountain Meadows Massacre in 1857. It has been described by scholars, historians, and eyewitnesses as the "darkest deed in the nineteenth century,"[3] and also happened to occur on September 11. Mountain Meadows was a point in Utah on the Old Spanish Trail leading west from Santa Fe, New Mexico. The Mormons who lived in this area experienced conflict with the government. Mormons are members of the Church of Jesus Christ of Latter Day Saints. Like many religious groups, they have extremists and can be misunderstood by the general public. Many Americans viewed them as devoted, if different, Christians, but some saw them as a dangerous cult.

The Mormon Church was feared and shunned by other Christian communities. This intolerance even included

This is a memorial to the victims of the Mountain Meadows Massacre of 1857.

violence, and law enforcement was no help because it was often involved in the persecution. By the late 1830s, the church's founder, Joseph Smith, and his followers were living in Nauvoo, Illinois, and had their own militia. Smith had an often hostile relationship with his neighbors, and he was killed by an angry mob. In his place, Brigham Young took over and led the Mormons to Utah.

At the time, Utah was outside the borders of the United States, so it was a perfect place to bring a group of marginalized people. Young became the territorial governor of Utah but ignored any instructions that the government gave him. Because of this, and because of his refusal to separate church and state, newly elected U.S. president James Buchanan decided to remove and replace Young. When Young heard of this plan, he instructed his people to stockpile ammunition and food, and he asked for help from nearby Native Americans in fighting for Mormonism.

Young became paranoid that any strangers might be spies for the government. A wagon train from Arkansas, which became known as the Baker-Fancher party, was traveling to California with 140 people at the same time a highly respected Mormon was murdered in Arkansas. There was no evidence that anyone in this party was involved in the murder, but there were rumors that they were responsible and also threatening violence against the Mormons in Utah. The Mormon militia, called the Nauvoo Legion, decided to arm the Native Americans in the area and encourage them to kill the entire Baker-Fancher party. Young was hundreds of miles away and later claimed he had discouraged the attack, but the militia started a gunfight anyway. On September 7, 1857, Paiutes and Mormons dressed as Paiutes opened fire on the travelers. This conflict lasted for days.

A Lethal Conclusion

On the fourth day, two Mormons approached the Baker-Fancher party and promised that if they surrendered their possessions, they would be escorted unharmed to Cedar City, Utah. Even though their possessions were all they had in the world, they agreed. They were led away from the sight of the battle, but Paiute fighters were waiting in ambush; 120 men, women, and children were slaughtered. Afterward, the Native Americans took all the possessions off the bodies, and the 17 children who were not killed—because they were under the age of 7—were taken to be raised in Mormon households. Later, Young acknowledged that he was partially responsible for this massacre, but he defended the actions of his followers: "I asked the Lord if it was all right for the deed to be done, to take the vision of the deed from my mind, and the Lord did so, and I feel first rate. It is all right. The only fear I have is from traitors."[4]

Despite his support of the Mormons' actions, Young submitted an official report blaming the Native Americans for the massacre and claimed the

Mormons were innocent. No one outside the Mormon community believed this. Still, a federal investigation did not take place until two years after the massacre. The investigation proved the blame for the killings should rest entirely on the Mormons. The children who had been kidnapped were returned to their families in Arkansas. No charges were filed against Young. Only one Mormon, John D. Lee, was tried and convicted. As a marginalized group, however, the Mormons had in fact committed America's first act of terrorism. In killing the entire Baker-Fancher party, they intended to intimidate and terrorize those who threatened their way of life.

The federal investigations into this massacre were continuously delayed or interrupted, first by the Utah War and then by the American Civil War. Lee was finally executed for the part he played in the event in 1877. This was the only concrete action the U.S. government took against the Mormons for their act of terrorism; however, Brigham Young did step down as territorial governor of Utah.

Luke Pryor Blackburn and the Yellow Fever Plot

Before John D. Lee was put to death for his involvement in the deaths of the Baker-Fancher party, another instance of terrorism was occurring elsewhere in the country. Luke Pryor Blackburn was a highly regarded medical doctor from Kentucky who focused his efforts on understanding and stopping the spread of infectious disease. He supported the South during the Civil War, and when the Confederacy was on the brink of defeat in 1864, Blackburn came up with a radical idea to defeat the Union. He hatched a plan to send clothing infected with yellow fever to cities in the North to make Union soldiers and civilians sick. When this plan was exposed, Dr. Blackburn became known as Dr. Black Vomit. This is one of the earliest examples of biological warfare and large-scale terrorism in American history—it has been reported that even Abraham Lincoln could have received one of the shipments of diseased clothing.

This example of terrorism is particularly scary because a man who was widely respected and trusted in the community carried it out, and because warfare that deals with disease is so difficult to predict, prevent, and control. This was especially true of yellow fever, which was extremely deadly during the 19th century. It was spread by mosquitos and caused fever, headache, and vomiting. Most who contracted it recovered after a few days, but a minority of cases lasted longer and became more serious—and sometimes fatal. The biggest problem with the disease was that symptoms did not appear until after the fever was contracted and spread to others.

Before the war, Blackburn had a reputation as a kind and gentle man—a doctor who would care for the sickest patients even if he was putting his own health at risk. He treated freed slaves and did not turn away patients who could not afford to pay him. He also channeled a

Luke Pryor Blackburn had the reputation of being a good doctor before he was revealed to be a Confederate terrorist.

lot of effort into studying yellow fever and attempting to control the spread of the disease with quarantine methods. When the Civil War started, however, Blackburn became a passionate supporter of the Confederacy. He wrote in an 1861 letter: "I hold every *Union traitor* as my enemy … I intend to begin the work of murder in earnest, and if I ever spare one of them, may hell be my portion. I want to see Union blood flow deep enough for my house to swim in it."[5]

Traveling Terror

To make his gruesome oaths a reality, Blackburn went to Bermuda in 1864 to collect clothing infected during a particularly nasty outbreak of yellow fever. He specifically wanted clothing stained with black vomit, which meant the wearer was suffering from the worst stage of the disease. He mixed the infected clothing with clean clothing, and shipped the clothes to Philadelphia, Pennsylvania; New York City; Washington, D.C.; and Norfolk, Virginia. Blackburn claimed that his diseased shipments were so powerful, they would devastate these northern stronghold cities. The hitch in Blackburn's attack came when his partner, Godfrey Hyams, became upset at not being paid for his role in the plan and reported the whole thing to the U.S. Consulate in Toronto, Canada.

Coincidentally, Hyams exposed the yellow fever plot the same day that Lincoln was assassinated, so Blackburn was suspected of both conspiracies. Blackburn hid in Canada until 1867, when a yellow fever epidemic broke out in the United States. He then wrote a letter to President Andrew Johnson, saying, "I have had much experience in the treatment of this disease and feel confident I could render essential service to my suffering and dying countrymen."[6] However, because of his previous attempted terrorist attack, his offer was refused. He still returned to America, where he lived until his death in 1887.

In the decades after Dr. Black Vomit was exposed, there have been speculations that Hyams exaggerated or even made up the story about the clothing infected with yellow fever. Because much evidence has been lost to history, it is hard to know if the infections would have helped the Confederate cause if the plan had succeeded. Blackburn's intentions, however, are labeled as terrorism because his passions and beliefs led him to take violent actions against those who disagreed with or posed a threat to his personal beliefs. Blackburn's intentions were to kill members of the the Union's military forces, but the intended use of a biological weapon meant that countless innocent civilians would have been affected. If Blackburn had been successful, members of the president's family might have been infected, as well as the postal employees who delivered the packages and anyone who happened to get too close to the clothing. Even those who would not become sick with the yellow fever would still be infected with the terror that came along with it.

Postwar Troubles Rising

Terrorism is often associated with an individual, such as Blackburn, or a small group, such as the Mormons of the Utah territory, fighting against a larger, established society using violence to communicate a message of intimidation. Not all cases of terrorism in American history are like this, however. The massacre in Colfax, Louisiana, in 1873 demonstrated the opposite circumstances: mainstream society using violence against a smaller group of people.

By 1873, the Civil War was over, but the country was still recovering from the deep wounds suffered during the conflict. Radical Republicans wanted to make freed slaves participants in politics and felt that Lincoln had not punished the South enough for seceding. The South was allowed to rejoin the Union with all property rights—which no longer included slaves. Radicals thought that the South would try to quietly reinstate slavery, especially after Lincoln's death. In an attempt to prevent slavery from being reinstated, two bills were introduced: They extended the life of the Freedmen's Bureau (the federal agency that helped free slaves integrate into American life) and included the Civil Rights Bill of 1866, which said that all people of any race (except Native American) born in the United States were citizens with equal benefits.

Johnson vetoed both bills. He wrote that "the distinction of race and color is, by the bill, made to operate in favor of the colored and against the white race."[7]

In response, Congress overrode the vetoes and passed the Civil Rights Act of 1866. However, because other politicians contested it, Republicans wanted to go directly to the U.S. Constitution. They wrote a new law establishing that black Americans would be full citizens and that those who had helped the South in the war would be forbidden from holding any government office. The law guaranteeing the citizenship of Americans regardless of race became known as the 14th Amendment to the Constitution. The Constitution can be amended if two-thirds of both houses of Congress submit a proposal and three-quarters of the states approve. In this case, both houses approved it, but there was a battle to get it ratified by the states.

Fighting the Amendment

Johnson was not quiet about his feelings about the amendment. The South also fought against it, but it was decided that if the states that disagreed wanted to rejoin the country, they would have to approve it. The South felt these laws were being forced on them. The fight between Johnson and Congress continued until Johnson became the first president to be impeached, but he was not removed from office. Ulysses S. Grant was elected president after Johnson's term ended. Despite Grant's pledge to both protect the freedmen and not alienate the South, trouble was already stirring. The Colfax Massacre occurred because of the South's feelings of resentment over the acknowledgment of the rights of black Americans.

President Johnson, shown here, was afraid that increased interracial relations would give black Americans too many rights.

After the Colfax Massacre, the wounded and the dead needed to be cared for, as shown here in this illustration.

Louisiana was one of the first states to surrender to the North, and it was not entirely peaceful. The state struggled with violence between Republicans and those who wanted to reinstate slavery. In 1873, two different men claimed to have been police chief of Grant Parish in Louisiana: an African American Union veteran William Ward, who was a former slave, and white Confederate veteran Christopher Columbus Nash. This caused a great deal of fighting until the Republicans who supported Ward took control of the parish courthouse in Colfax and remained there to keep out white supremacists who were preparing to force their candidate into power. This action made local white residents angry because the newly free blacks were starting to stand up for their civil liberties and equal rights.

Nash began planning a full attack against Ward and those in the courthouse. When he demanded that the black Americans surrender and they refused, he gave them 30 minutes to release the women and children before he started firing at the building. When this proved to be ineffective, he reportedly rolled up a cannon to shoot at the building, which caused many supporters to abandon the cause. Nash's men followed them and shot most of them. Then, a black prisoner was forced to set fire to the entire courthouse itself. Once the building was burning, the Republicans began flying white flags of surrender. However, when a white supremacist was shot by one of Ward's men, the angry whites ignored those white flags and killed everyone they could—including those who tried to run away. In total, 150 African Americans and 3 whites were killed during the fighting.

This massacre was a frightening realization that the South was far from being reformed into an area safe for—let alone friendly to—African Americans. The tradition of white supremacy would not easily be erased. The U.S. government caught those white supremacists, but they were considered local heroes for their actions. Nearly 100 individuals were formally charged for their actions, and 9 of those ended up being convicted for violating the Enforcement Act of 1870, which was passed to ensure that citizens were not denied their constitutional rights. During the trials, more than 100 people came forward to describe the scene at the Colfax courthouse, and many of these witnesses were beaten or intimidated by their neighbors.

Despite overwhelming evidence that dozens of white men in Colfax were responsible for more than 100 African American deaths during the massacre, no one served a sentence for murder. The few men who were convicted had their cases thrown out when the Supreme Court ruled that the Enforcement Act was unconstitutional. Because local authorities were supportive of white supremacy, neither the state of Louisiana nor the town of Colfax pressed further charges against the men responsible.

History sees the Colfax Massacre as an act of terrorism because Nash used the incident as a warning—and an intimidation tactic—against those who might want to stand up for African American liberties and freedoms. In 1874, Nash formed the White League, a racist group that operated openly and without fear of punishment. His group and those like it—such as the Ku Klux Klan (KKK)—used violence to terrorize leaders among the former slaves and the white Republicans who supported them. The white elites were the terrorists in this scenario. Racist terrorism still rages across America, carried out by both whites and minority groups.

Chapter Two

TERRORISM IN 20TH CENTURY AMERICA

After the Civil War shattered the United States and sparked racial tension across the country, most people were ready to move on to the next stage of American development. With the turn of the 20th century came new technology, including the steam engine, industrialization, and automobiles. It also introduced new weapons with which to carry out acts of terrorism. As explosive material—formerly only available to wealthy purchasers, such as the U.S. government—became more common and scientists came up with new ways to make bombs, violent criminals turned to using homemade bombs to commit acts of terror.

An Explosive Time

On October 1, 1910, an explosion ripped through the offices of the *Los Angeles Times*, killing 21 people. A member of the International Association of Bridge and Structural Workers had placed dynamite at the newspaper's building. It was one of the first high-profile cases of violence in the new century—but at least half a dozen other criminal acts of violence were also identified as being closely aligned with terrorism.

The 1900s saw a good deal of violence that arose from labor disputes between workers and employers. Working conditions were described as dangerous and degrading while compensation was not enough to live on. Employers denied these accusations and insisted that the conditions were safe and the pay was appropriate for the type or amount of work. In the fall of 1910, Los Angeles metalworkers went on strike, and the owner of the *Times*, Harrison Gray Otis, publicly opposed it. Otis considered himself an anti-union man and wanted to give a voice to the employers. This, unsurprisingly, was upsetting to the metalworkers

This image shows the destruction after the bombing of Los Angeles Times.

who were fighting for a better life.

Unlike other acts of terrorism before or since, the bombing of the *Times* was not necessarily intended to cause casualties. It has been speculated that the terrorists only wanted to send a message by destroying property—not by taking anyone's life. However, there were employees in the offices when the bomb went off. The southern wall of the building collapsed, causing the floors to give way under the weight of the printing presses. When the building collapsed, the gas mainline was ignited. The investigators also found a bomb at Otis's home, but they were able to remove it safely.

Unlike earlier instances of terrorism in U.S. history, in the aftermath of the *Times* bombing, the government actively sought out an individual to blame and bring to justice. A private detective—William J. Burns—was hired by the local city government, which realized the best way to find out who was guilty of this act of terrorism was to become friendly with Otis's enemies. In this case, the laboring metalworkers in the Los Angeles area were the most likely suspects. By targeting the investigation as such, Burns identified three men who were recognized by witnesses as being in the area of the bombing. Ortie McManigal, a member of the union, eventually confessed that he was aware that John J. McNamara was the mastermind behind the plot, alongside his brother, James.

Laboring for Labor

Pro-labor organizations collected $50,000 to pay for a criminal defense lawyer for the McNamara brothers. This lawyer was Clarence Darrow, a man with a reputation as a champion of the working class. The brothers faced a number of serious criminal charges but pled not guilty to all of them. Darrow described his clients as the victims of unfair labor laws and a bullying prosecution, not murderers. Because the McNamaras had support from California's working class, which could cause the jury to act unpredictably, both Darrow and the prosecutor, John Fredericks, agreed to a compromise: The brothers would plead guilty and avoid death sentences. James would receive a life sentence, while John was given a much shorter term.

The problem with this compromise was that it seemed like a rather lenient punishment—some officials were worried that future potential bombers could be encouraged. Moreover, pro-labor organizations felt betrayed—they had come up with money to pay for the best defense lawyer and had been forced to settle for a plea of guilty.

The brothers served the time they were sentenced to. James died in prison. Although John got out after 10 years, he died the same year as his brother, in 1941. Their bombing was an act of terrorism because it used violence to communicate a strong political statement: The working class would not silently accept abuse from those in power. Though they may have started out with good intentions, the brothers were still guilty of committing an act of terrorism, which is wrong regardless of intent.

The Wall Street Bombing

Ten years after the *Los Angeles Times* bombing, a horse-drawn carriage rode up to 23 Wall Street in New York City carrying hundreds of pounds of metal and explosives. This bomb exploded at noon on September 16, 1920, at the center of the country's financial power. The explosion was meant to destroy and kill; glass was blown out of windows in a half-mile radius. Those working in the financial district described the sound as extremely loud and the impact as frightening. The carriage and horses were completely annihilated.

This bombing was the work of a terrorist who wanted to send a message of hate and resentment to those in positions of wealth and power—and he succeeded. Even veterans of World War I were recorded as saying they had never seen the amount of suffering that this explosion caused. The New York Stock Exchange closed, and panic over the possibility of a second explosion grew. Nearly 40 people had been killed, and it was difficult to identify the bodies. More than 200 people were seriously injured.

Once it became clear that there was not going to be an immediate follow-up explosion, some thought it had been an accident. However, there was no report of missing dynamite anywhere nearby, so it was ruled a deliberate action. One of the first investigators to study the scene was William J. Burns, who had helped find the *Times* bombers. He said, "There is not the slightest doubt that it was a bomb which caused the explosion … From my investigation I am certain that the bomb was in the wagon which was destroyed."[8] William J. Flynn became the lead investigator for the case and said anarchists were to blame. Flynn came from the Bureau of Investigation (what is now the FBI) and was not interested in being a celebrity or making headlines. He was a serious man who wanted to figure out who committed the crime, gather enough evidence to convict them,

When the Wall Street bomb went off, cars were destroyed, and debris was everywhere.

and put the terrorist behind bars.

Fighting Back

Soon after the bombing, flyers were found in a nearby mailbox. They read: "Remember we will not tolerate any longer. Free the political prisoners or it will be sure death for all of you."[9] This frightening message was signed by the American Anarchist Fighters. The threat that anarchists posed in 1920 was similar to the threat many feel from extremist groups in the 21st century. Anarchists, communists, and extremists symbolized the destruction of the American way of life. In fact, this is exactly what extremist Muslims were aiming to accomplish by following the orders of Osama bin Laden in the 1990s and 2000s. In 1920, the American public preferred the comforts of law and order over the social change that political radicals represented.

Although many self-identified anarchists were investigated, none were found to be responsible. After failing to come up with any solid suspects in New York, Flynn widened the search to include the entire county—and a $100,000 reward was offered for any information that led to arrests. The director of the FBI, J. Edgar Hoover, became obsessed with the case and trying to solve it. He was always willing to follow new leads, no matter how improbable. Despite media attention and public fear, no one was charged with the crime, and the case officially closed in 1940.

At the time, this attack was the first of its kind—deliberate violence meant to kill as many as possible, including innocent bystanders. The bombing was the birth of a new kind of domestic terrorism in the United States. There is a good chance that it was a suicide bombing, since the bomber must have been close by to ignite the carriage full of explosives. This also posed a new problem for the government to combat. It is extremely difficult to prevent a suicide bomber: Law enforcement must anticipate every move and predict when and where a suicide bombing might happen. Moreover, modern suicide bombers can conceal small bombs—with massive destructive power—underneath clothing, making them nearly impossible to see.

This act of terrorism had a strong effect on police work, reshaping it to what it is today. The anonymous suicide bomber that intends to kill hundreds of innocent people is not motivated in the same way other criminals might be. Because of this, crimes of terror need to be handled differently in how the terrorists are charged, tried, and convicted. The idea is to prevent similar acts of terrorism from being committed. The Wall Street bombing demonstrated that traditional police procedures are not the most effective way of solving cases of terrorism.

A Baptist Church and Civil Rights

The civil rights movement brought to light the racial problems that have existed in the United States for centuries. Although black people were no longer

Emma Goldman

The most famous anarchist at the time of the Wall Street bombing was Emma Goldman. Goldman was born in Russia, but moved to New York City in 1885 as a teenager. She wrote articles and gave speeches that encouraged union workers to fight back against the management, even if that meant using violence. Those who admired and followed her believed she was a brave champion of individualism. In their eyes, she had made large personal sacrifices to be a voice for the common working person. To many, however, she symbolized chaos. She encouraged a dangerously disruptive force that could tear apart society and the country. She was never officially accused of the bombing, despite public belief she may have been behind it.

Emma Goldman was a radical political figure in the 19th and 20th centuries. Many believed she was responsible for the Wall Street attack.

slaves, they continued to be marginalized and oppressed because of prejudice in the larger society. Citizens who fear change and difference lash out at what they think to be the source of that change—for racist whites, that means attacking blacks.

Many occurrences of racial unrest during the 1960s were terribly violent. Black people felt their rights were being denied in favor of white comfort, and whites responded with violence. The 1968 assassination of Dr. Martin Luther King Jr., who stood for peace and unity, was an extreme example of this violence. Before King was killed, the 16th Street Baptist Church bombing in Birmingham, Alabama, stands out as a particularly brutal incident of terrorism.

The civil rights movement was simply trying to win basic American rights for black people—who were citizens just like the white majority. Those who opposed this accused King and other leaders of being a threat to the United States and the American dream. When four innocent children were killed in the 16th Street Baptist Church bombing, a terrorist act carried out by white supremacists, it "revealed the inequities in the treatment of black citizens in a way that no organized march or rowdy protest or fiery speech ever could."[10]

On September 15, 1963, four girls were killed in a dynamite explosion at the church. Members of the United Klans of America, a branch of the KKK, planted the dynamite. More than 20 people were injured in the explosion; one girl permanently lost her sight in one eye. Immediately after the blast, black community members and police in riot gear were on the scene. The girls who were killed were Denise McNair (11 years old), Addie Mae Collins (14), Carole Robertson (14), and Cynthia Wesley (14). Four innocent girls died because of the hatred of white extremists. This is a key element of terrorism, and one reason why it is so scary: There could be devastating violence anywhere at any time. It panics people and makes them afraid to go about their daily lives. The 16th Street Baptist Church had become a symbol of the growing black middle class in Birmingham—King had given a speech there the previous spring, applauding the community's efforts—and the KKK was trying to prevent this group of people from thriving by killing them.

Trouble Down South

The threat of violence in Birmingham was especially bad because of how infamous the city's police chief and Alabama's governor were for their racist language and defense of white supremacy. When he was sworn in, Governor George Wallace said, "In the name of the greatest people that have ever trod this earth [whites], I draw a line in the dust and toss the gauntlet before the feet of tyranny, and I say, segregation now, segregation tomorrow, and segregation forever."[11] It is difficult to fight terrorism fueled by racism when elected officials publicly support hatred and division. This kind of divisive language coming from a public figure only made the problem worse.

Martin Luther King Jr. was one of the most important figures in the civil rights movement.

J. Edgar Hoover

Hoover was the first director of the FBI once it was renamed in 1935. (It was originally the Bureau of Investigation.) Hoover is recognized for making the FBI a more efficient crime-fighting organization. Despite his accomplishments as an investigator, there are arguments that Hoover abused his power. He sometimes used his position to harass those who disagreed with him politically, and he sometimes collected evidence illegally. President Harry S. Truman claimed that Hoover made the FBI into his own private police force. Presidents Truman, John F. Kennedy, and Richard Nixon all considered removing Hoover as director of the FBI but decided against it for political reasons.

J. Edgar Hoover oversaw the transition of the Bureau of Investigation into the Federal Bureau of Investigation.

Not everyone participated in or was aware of the issues facing blacks in the southern states. For these citizens, the news of children being killed in bomb explosions or images of Birmingham's police chief ordering his men to blast peaceful black protesters with fire hoses was horrific—and demonstrated how brutal white supremacy is.

The FBI arrived to the scene of the explosion very quickly, despite the fact that the chief, J. Edgar Hoover, was not known for his sympathy toward civil rights activists. Because this was a major act of terrorism, the FBI had no choice but to investigate immediately. Despite the FBI's speedy arrival, and despite the emergence of four white supremacists as suspects, Hoover did not follow through on civil rights cases, and the case was closed in 1968. It was reopened in 1971 by Alabama attorney general Bill Baxley, and in 1977, one of those white supremacists, Robert Chambliss, was charged and convicted of murder. Of the other three, one died before he could be charged, and two were not convicted until the 21st century.

Although it took almost 40 years for

This memorial to the victims of the 16th Street Baptist Church bombing is a symbol of resistance to old racist ideas and a reminder of the dangers of terrorism.

America's Most Infamous Racists

The KKK was created by former Confederate soldiers after the Civil War. Its main belief was that black people should be kept below white people through any means necessary—including, and especially, violence. They placed a particular emphasis on Christian values that appealed to conservative white southerners raised in heavily religious households. The KKK did not just hate black people. They extended their hate to Catholics, Jews, and any foreigner who they thought threatened the Christian principles of "true Americans," which they believed themselves to be. When the 16th Street Baptist Church bombing occurred, the KKK was not one big united organization; instead, it was multiple smaller groups with racism in common.

the last two men to be convicted, it does show that acts of terrorism will not escape justice indefinitely. While it seems outrageous that four children could be killed without anyone being immediately held responsible, prosecutors have since made an effort to reopen such cases to ensure that justice prevails.

Counterculture Movement

During the civil rights movement, there was also the countercultural movement across the United States. In the South, some whites were suspicious of African Americans, and all over the country, the younger generations were suspicious of the government. The Vietnam War, which dragged on from 1955 to 1975, generated countless anti-government organizations run by young activists. These activists were considered "countercultural" because they tried to go against, or counter, the widespread culture in America—which they viewed as violent, money-hungry, and too conservative. Most of these organizations were peaceful, since peace was the action they were trying to promote, but not all embraced this message.

The Weather Underground, or Weathermen, declared war on the government. They insisted that if the United States was going to export violence overseas, then a resistance movement would bring violence to them at home. The organization wanted to force the government to end the war in Vietnam and thought a working class revolution was the way to do so. They believed nonviolent protests were not getting the job done. They were sure that violence could force the government to change its views and actions. In other

Days of Rage

The "Days of Rage" were a series of demonstrations that the Weather Underground carried out in October 1969 in Chicago. They were meant to call attention to elections and the violence the government was promoting overseas in the Vietnam War. The group called it "National Action," and its slogan was "Bring the war home." Bringing the war home meant vandalizing homes, businesses, and cars. They also assaulted police officers. Dozens were hurt, and nearly 300 members of the Weather Underground were arrested. Overall, the turnout for the protests was low, and the police presence was high, which ended up causing more violence than the organization had intended. These riots cost Illinois $183,000 in damages, and the Weather Underground paid more than $243,000 in bail money.

words, they wanted to use terrorism for political reform.

The Weathermen carried out multiple bombings in the 1960s and 1970s. In October 1969, the organization took credit for bombing a statue in Chicago, Illinois. This attack did not seriously harm any civilians, but the statue was targeted because it was a memorial to violent police action in 1886. One year later, after the statue had been repaired, they blew it up again. It was in that same year, 1970, that the Weather Underground began focusing their efforts on causing physical harm and death. In February, a bomb loaded with nails—designed to shoot out like bullets when it exploded—was put on a window ledge of a San Francisco police station, killing one officer and wounding another. Though the group did not claim credit for this attack, they were the likely suspects. Five days later, members of the Weather Underground attempted to commit arson on the house of John M. Murtagh, a state supreme court justice in New York. This attack failed, however, and Murtagh and his family were able to escape the blaze unharmed.

Shutting Down the Underground

The Weather Underground continued to manufacture bombs and plan terrorist attacks across the country. While making more nail bombs, one exploded accidentally and killed three Weathermen. This accidental explosion was what really captured the attention of the media and the public, and it caused the leaders of the organization to go into hiding. They

A Presidential Connection?

One former leader of the Weather Underground was Bill Ayers, who was known in the 1960s for his activism and then, later in life, for his work in education reform. Long after the organization folded, Ayers ended up in the same circles as influential politicians in Chicago, such as Barack Obama. This connection was public knowledge in Chicago, but conservative newspapers picked up the story. This became material for Obama's opponents in the presidential race, who accused Obama of having links to terrorism. Ayers denied any close relationship with Obama and criticized Republicans—the loudest Obama opponents—for assuming he was guilty just by being mildly associated with someone with a troubled past.

---

remained relatively quiet for a few years. Then, in May 1972, they placed a bomb in a women's bathroom in the Pentagon. This was a high-profile attack, striking at the heart of America's military power, but it still did not gain the group much political traction. In November 1977, after the Vietnam War had ended, five members of the Weather Underground were arrested for plans to bomb a California senator who supported nuclear power. After these arrests, the organization ceased to exist.

Although the number of casualties caused by the organization was low, the FBI correctly labeled them as a domestic terrorist group. Despite this label, the FBI was never able to fully prosecute the Weathermen because a lot of the information that investigators gathered was obtained through illegal surveillance. Though the Weather Underground did not last long, its members acknowledged that their efforts were just the beginning. They called their actions a "a bee sting against such a powerful enemy, but a bee sting whose strength is multiplied many times by the fact that these actions represent the early stages of sustained armed struggle led by a political organization."[12] The Weathermen considered themselves heroes and patriots, fighting for a better government. However, like most terrorist groups, their ideals were distorted by violence. The armed struggle they described would be carried out by other groups of anti-government terrorists throughout the 20th century.

Chapter Three

DOMESTIC BOMBINGS

The mid-to-late 20th century was a challenging and unstable time in the United States. From the assassination of President John F. Kennedy to the Vietnam War, political controversy and social upheaval were the definitive features of the 1960s, 1970s, and 1980s. With increasing technological advances, including rocket science and computer technologies, millions of Americans were seeing the world—and their lifestyles—change right before their eyes. While most people welcomed these advances, some reacted angrily—and violently. These terrorists continued some of the aggressive tactics displayed in the earlier decades 20th century, including the use of bombs and targeting innocent people as well as political opponents.

Ted Kaczynski

Ted Kaczynski, one of America's most infamous criminals, embraced the ideals of anti-authority that the Weather Underground promoted in the 1960s and 1970s. He was 53 years old when he was captured by the FBI for killing 3 people and injuring more than 20 over a span of 18 years. Kaczynski, nicknamed the Unabomber by media and authorities because his first bombs were associated with universities and airplanes, had caused the longest and most expensive manhunt in U.S. history. He was finally arrested in 1996.

Kaczynski had problems socializing and forming healthy relationships. Historians and therapists have speculated that these issues stemmed from his unusual childhood. When he was six months old, he was hospitalized periodically for several months due to a severe allergic reaction to medication, and his family was not allowed to visit him. When he came home, he was physically healthy but unresponsive emotionally. According to his mother, this uncaring personality

As a young man, Ted Kaczynski was a rising star in the academic world.

increased as he got older and was accompanied by rage. Despite his psychological troubles, Kaczynski was extremely intelligent, reading and composing music from a young age, but he avoided other children. He claimed his troubles were caused by his parents and self-imposed academic pressures, but his mother and brother insisted that his family life was relatively happy and normal.

After skipping a few grades in high school, Kaczynski was accepted into Harvard University when he was just 16 years old. His high school guidance counselor wrote to Harvard: "I believe Ted has one of the greatest contributions to make to society. He is reflective, sensitive, and deeply conscious of his responsibilities to society ... His only drawback is a tendency to be rather quiet in his original meetings with people."[13] At the university, he was put in a freshman dorm specifically for the most promising incoming students. In his unpublished autobiography, he insisted that Harvard was great for him, that he learned self-discipline, swam, wrestled, and even came out of his shell to make some friends.

During his studies at Harvard, Kaczynski was involved as a test subject in a series of experiments at the Henry A. Murray Research Center. These experiments were conducted as a way to measure how people react differently under stress. Murray himself would verbally attack the subjects and record how they responded. Historians have questioned whether this experiment had an adverse effect on Kaczynski. When he was on trial for murder, a forensic psychiatrist examined him and wrote that Kaczynski "has intertwined his two belief systems, that society is bad and he should rebel against it, and his intense anger at his family for his perceived injustices."[14] He told the psychiatrist that it was during college that he first felt like he had to completely break away from society.

Kaczynski graduated from Harvard in 1962 when he was 20, and he was accepted into a top graduate program for mathematical study at the University of Michigan. After earning his Ph.D. in 1967, the University of California, Berkeley, offered him a job as an assistant professor. He accepted, but by 1969, angrier and more antisocial, he had moved back home with his parents. He claimed that most of his students wanted to become engineers, creating technology that would destroy the environment, which he wanted nothing to do with. At home, he had a few low-level jobs before moving to Montana, where he lived on a piece of land with no electricity, plumbing, or neighbors. Seven years later, a bomb went off in Chicago.

The Unabomber

On May 25, 1978, a brown package was discovered in a parking lot at the University of Illinois. It was addressed to a professor of rocket science at the Rensselaer Polytechnic Institute, which is located in Troy, New York. The sender was written as Buckley Crist Jr., a professor at the nearby Northwestern University. As a result, the person who discovered the package tried to deliver it back to the sender. However, Crist did not send this package—and when he had a security guard inspect it, it blew up. The security guard suffered only light wounds because the bomb was made of wood instead of metal. After the authorities investigated the package, they closed the case because no one had been seriously injured. In May 1979, a box was left on a table at Northwestern Technological Institute. When a student tried to open it, it exploded, giving him cuts and burns. After this bombing, authorities took more notice—there were now two attacks in a similar location. They recognized the similarities between the two bombs. However, they did not have enough information to pursue suspects.

Later that same year, a bomb was found in the cargo hold of an American Airlines flight taking off from Chicago for Washington, D.C. The bomb did not explode but did catch fire, filling the plane with smoke. If it had exploded, it would have destroyed the plane, and most of the passengers would have died or suffered serious injuries. When the FBI investigated this bomb, it had such unique features that it was easily linked to the first two bombs, which had also originated in the Chicago area. The FBI put together a task force whose job was to inspect the bomb fragments and examine the victims. Their goal was to determine the motive of the bomber or bombers.

Kaczynski was hard to track. Because he was a respected intellectual, he did not fit the stereotypical mold for a terrorist. He did not frequently venture from his Montana cabin to use credit cards or interact with anyone. He waited for long stretches between attacks and seemingly acted at random. The conventional ways that law enforcement investigated terrorists were not very helpful in his case because he stayed off the grid.

The FBI made no headway, and Kaczynski continued his bombing. In June 1980, a hollowed-out book with an explosive in it was sent to the president of United Airlines. Once again, it only caused minor injuries. An FBI agent then created a psychological profile of the Unabomber. Law enforcement agencies create these profiles—which speculate the age, gender, and personality of high-profile criminals—as a way to narrow suspects down. It concluded that the terrorist was very intelligent and opposed to technology; both of these speculations turned out to be correct.

Meanwhile, Kaczynski was upset that he had not yet killed anyone, writing in his diary: "Frustrating that I can't seem to make a lethal bomb."[15] Over the next few years, three bombs connected to Kaczynski appeared. In 1981, a worker found an explosive device in Utah, which was successfully defused by local police. In 1982, however, two more serious incidents occurred: In Tennessee, a professor's secretary suffered serious injuries, and in California, a professor of computer science was nearly killed. The Unabomber then stayed quiet for three years before his next series of attacks.

In 1985, a student at the University of California, Berkeley, was seriously injured in a blast caused by a bomb hidden in a package in the computer science lab; he lost most of the use of his right arm. Later that year, another student was injured when he opened a package intended for a professor of psychology at the University of Michigan.

Then, in December of 1985, Kaczynski claimed his first fatality. The owner of a computer store in California was killed in his parking lot by a disguised nail bomb. The FBI recognized the style of bomb as being similar to the others. When Kaczynski learned he had succeeded in taking someone's life, he wrote, "Excellent. Humane way to eliminate somebody. He probably never felt a thing. $25,000 award offered. Rather flattering."[16] In early 1987, Kaczynski tried to recreate that attack with another computer store bombing. This time, the shop owner was only injured—and Kaczynski, the infamous Unabomber, was seen by a passer-by. A drawing was made by the FBI and released to the public, but the eyewitness claimed it did not look enough like the Unabomber, and the FBI still had no solid leads.

The Unabomber Improves

Six years passed after the 1987 attack, and the FBI hoped that the Unabomber had disappeared on his own. Kaczynski kept a low profile and refined his bombs to make them more lethal. In June 1993, two professors—one from the University of California, San Francisco, and one from Yale—received bombs in the mail. Both were seriously injured but not killed.

Because so much time had passed, the FBI and local police thought this might be the work of a copycat bomber, or someone trying to mimic the actions of the real Unabomber. A few days after these bombings, Kaczynski sent a letter to the *New York Times*, claiming to be a member of a group named FC (short for Freedom Club) that was killing people it deemed harmful to the future of humanity. However, this was later revealed to be a lie; Kaczynski never worked as a member of any organization. It has been speculated that he pretended to be part of a group to further hide his identity.

In December 1994, a New York advertising executive, Thomas Mosser, received a package in the mail. When he opened it, the package exploded and killed him in his home. A few months after this attack, the Unabomber claimed credit: "Through our bombings we hope to promote social instability in industrial society, propagate anti-industrial ideas and give encouragement to those who hate the industrial system."[17] Kaczynski used "we" to further trick people into believing he was part of an organization. Some historians have claimed that he used "we" to imply that many Americans felt the same way he did—and that those who represented mainstream society should fear for their lives. Kaczynski went on to call the FBI a weak and ineffective organization. He claimed that he was not afraid of being discovered or apprehended. He also described himself as someone who did not want to commit acts of terror, insisting that making bombs all the time was

Despite being seen at his 1987 bombing, which led to this sketch, the Unabomber was still able to avoid capture for nearly another decade.

In His Own Words

Kaczynski kept a journal that detailed his attacks. By examining his diary, psychologists and historians have been able to dissect what may have been going on in his mind as he carried out his crimes. Psychologists have concluded that he was severely mentally ill and most likely suffered from schizophrenia, a mental disease that causes people to have delusions and act aggressively. In the following passage, Kaczynski seems to acknowledge that his actions suggest a mental illness—but he also wrote that he is perfectly healthy. This kind of delusion is also a symptom of schizophrenia.

I intend to start killing people. If I am successful at this, it is possible that, when I am caught (not alive, I fervently hope!) there will be some speculation in the news media as to my motives for killing … If some speculation occurs, they are bound to make me out to be a sickie, and to ascribe to me motives of a sordid or "sick" type. Of course, the term "sick" in such a context represents a value judgment … the news media may have something to say about me when I am killed or caught. And they are bound to try to [analyze] my psychology and depict me as "sick." This powerful bias should be borne [in mind] in reading any attempts to [analyze] my psychology.[1]

1. Quoted in Alston Chase, "Harvard and the Making of the Unabomber," *The Atlantic*, June 2000. www.theatlantic.com/magazine/archive/2000/06/harvard-and-the-making-of-the-unabomber/378239/.

not something he enjoyed, but something that had to be done.

The last victim of the Unabomber was Gilbert Murray, a lobbyist working for the California Forestry Association. The bomb was mailed to his office and killed him immediately after it was opened. It turned out that the bomb was actually addressed to the man who had Murray's job before him, but in a letter to the *New York Times*, Kaczynski wrote, "We have no regret about the fact that our bomb blew up the wrong man … he was pursuing the same goals."[18] As with many victims of terrorist attacks, those injured and killed by the Unabomber were chosen because of what they supposedly represented, not who they were as individual people.

In June 1995, Kaczynski wrote a

manuscript and sent it to several national news publications, including the *New York Times*. It was accompanied by a note that said: "If the enclosed manuscript is published reasonably soon and receives wide public exposure, we will permanently desist from terrorism."[19] By September of that year, both the *New York Times* and *Washington Post* had published the Unabomber's 56-page manuscript, which they called his manifesto. It detailed how dangerous technology and advances in science are to humankind. The anti-government and anti-technology ideas made sense to a lot of Americans, who felt the government had too much power. One journalist for *TIME* magazine wrote, "There's a little bit of the Unabomber in most of us."[20]

The manifesto was meant to reach as many Americans as possible, including Kaczynski's brother, David, who recognized the writing style as Ted's. The brothers had not spoken in years. David sent copies of letters that Ted had written to a private investigator to be compared to the style of writing of the manifesto. The private investigator handed these samples over to the FBI. David agreed to help the FBI capture his brother as long as he did not receive the death penalty—the FBI then went to Montana, where David knew his brother spent most of his time in his remote cabin.

Kaczynski's cabin was raided on April 3, 1996. The FBI found a bomb-making factory and multiple notebooks full of inventions, plans, and confessions. A federal grand jury indicted him on several counts of murder, attempted murder, and other serious crimes. Kaczynski's attorneys wanted to plead insanity—against their client's wishes—so he fired them and decided to represent himself. Kaczynski's family, meanwhile, did all they could to portray him to the public as a brilliant—but clearly troubled—man who was a victim of society. They argued that he did not deserve the death penalty, despite his nearly two decades of terrorism. Kaczynski agreed to plead guilty to the charges brought against him, which would avoid a long and brutal trial, in exchange for life in prison instead of execution. He was sentenced to life in prison without the possibility of parole (meaning he can never be released) in 1998. Kaczynski believed that the government's powers were too strong, education was untrustworthy, and entertainment was meant to make people unintelligent and unquestioning. He felt he had to destroy this system. As with many terrorists, however, he failed to do so, and he destroyed other people's lives instead.

Oklahoma City and Timothy McVeigh

Before the September 11 attacks, the worst domestic terrorist attack in U.S. history took place on April 19, 1995. The Alfred P. Murrah Federal Building in Oklahoma City, Oklahoma, was bombed, killing 168 people and injuring more than 500. Of those killed, 19 were children at the on-site day care center; only 6 children survived. The man responsible for this attack—a shocking

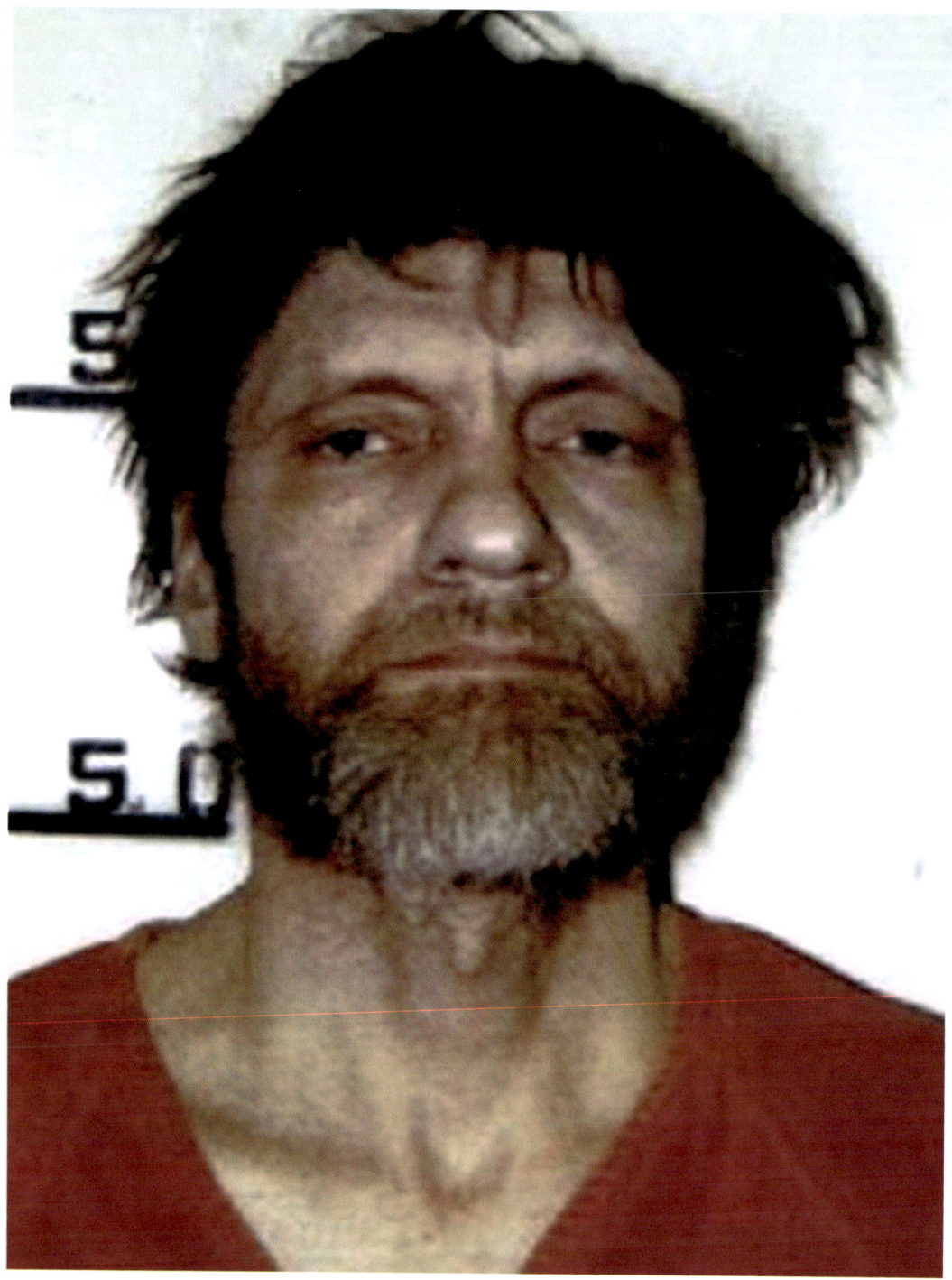

Kaczynski, shown here in first mug shot when he was finally caught in 1996, was similar in some ways to Timothy McVeigh.

A Manifesto

Most of Kaczynski's attacks were motivated by powerful anti-government and anti-technology ideas that he had been nurturing for most of his life. Much of his manifesto is dedicated to describing the dangers of increasing technology and industrialism in America and across the world:

The Industrial Revolution and its consequences have been a disaster for the human race. They have greatly increased the life-expectancy of those of us who live in "advanced" countries, but they have destabilized society, have made life unfulfilling, have subjected human beings to indignities, have led to widespread psychological suffering (in the Third World to physical suffering as well) and have inflicted severe damage on the natural world. The continued development of technology will worsen the situation. It will certainly subject human beings to greater indignities and inflict greater damage on the natural world, it will probably lead to greater social disruption and psychological suffering, and it may lead to increased physical suffering even in "advanced" countries.[1]

1. Ted Kaczynski, "Industrial Society and Its Future," *Washington Post*, September 22, 1995. www.washingtonpost.com/wp-srv/national/longterm/unabomber/manifesto.text.htm.

---

and horrifying moment in American history—was Timothy McVeigh, an anti-government radical terrorist.

In some ways, McVeigh was similar to Kaczynski—he was intelligent, kept to himself, had a tough childhood, and believed the government was getting too powerful. McVeigh's grandfather was a strong presence in his life and taught him how to shoot guns and defend himself. After he dropped out of college, McVeigh worked a few low-level jobs before enlisting in the U.S. Army. At first, he was a successful soldier, even receiving a Bronze Star for bravery.

McVeigh fought in the Gulf War. He was sure he would die in the conflict, and his bitterness toward the government grew when he saw American soldiers looting Iraqi homes. McVeigh was selected to join the U.S. Army Special Forces, but he dropped out the training. This only contributed to his resentment toward the United States. In 1991, he left the military, joined the KKK, and probably suffered from post–traumatic stress disorder (PTSD). He began to spend a lot of time with friends he met in the army, Terry Nichols and Michael Fortier, and started writing angry letters to congressmen and newspapers. He even believed that the army had implanted a microchip in him so they could track his movements.

In 1993, after traveling with Nichols and Fortier as a gun salesman, McVeigh was in Waco, Texas, during the Branch Davidian raid. The Branch Davidians were a small religious congregation that

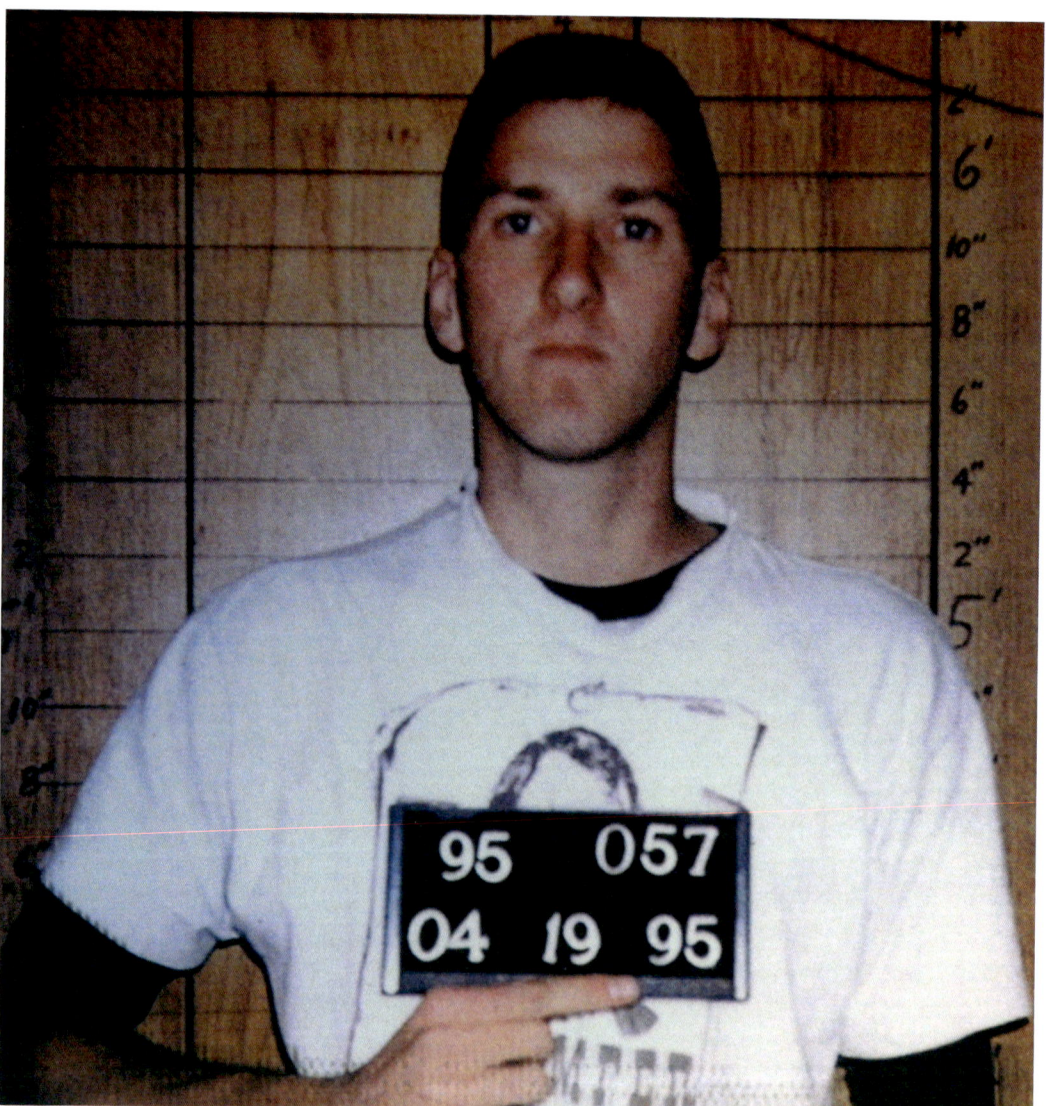

Timothy McVeigh was similar to many terrorists: He believed he was fighting for a noble cause, even though he was a mass murderer.

had, in the years leading up to the raid, come under scrutiny for their alleged child abuse and illegal weapons sales. Many viewed them as a dangerous cult that could harm the Waco community. Beginning in February 1993, several federal agencies, including the FBI, worked together to infiltrate their compound, named Mount Carmel, and arrest Branch Davidian members. However, the situation quickly escalated, and the result was a nearly two-month standoff that lasted until Mount Carmel was burned to the ground on April 19. During the extended raid, 80 Branch Davidians and some federal officers were killed. McVeigh joined in watching the standoff.

After the way the FBI handled the case, McVeigh became motivated to act on his anti-government feelings. He said, "The government is afraid of the guns people have because they have to have control of the people at all times. Once you take away the guns, you can do anything to the people ... The government is continually growing bigger and more powerful, and the people need to prepare to defend themselves against governmental control."[21] Working and planning alongside Nichols, he began buying fertilizer in large amounts for making bombs. McVeigh wanted to make a statement and capture headlines with an act of violence against the government. To do this, he felt he needed a high body count; he aimed to make the weapon as destructive as possible and looked for a location that would cause outrage.

A Deadly Plan

McVeigh decided to target a federal building: the Alfred P. Murrah Federal Building in Oklahoma City. He wanted to kill FBI agents in particular. On April 19, 1995, McVeigh packed a truck full of explosives but waited to drive it to his targeted building until after rush hour. He wanted to make sure that all employees would be working at their desks when the explosion ripped through their offices. He parked the truck, lit a five-minute fuse, and walked away. Six witnesses say they saw him that morning.

When the bomb went off just after 9 a.m., more than 300 buildings in the area were damaged. A hole was torn into the building, causing several floors to collapse and crush people. Of the 168 people killed, 8 were federal agents, and most worked in some capacity for the federal government. McVeigh later claimed he was not aware that he had parked so close to the building's day care, killing so many children. When he learned of this fact, he simply regarded it as a cost of sending his message; he was not remorseful.

After the explosion, volunteers and rescue workers rushed to the scene. Even with so many to help, it was difficult to identify the victims. President Bill Clinton declared a state of emergency and sent an investigative team. McVeigh fled the scene in his car, but a state trooper pulled him over for a license plate violation. During this traffic stop, the officer discovered that McVeigh was carrying a handgun for which he had no license. The officer arrested him on the weapon

Inspired by the Branch

The Branch Davidians were a small religious community led by David Koresh, a self-proclaimed prophet. The 1993 raid of Mount Carmel was caused by a former member's allegations of child abuse and other criminal activities within the group. Though federal investigators could have obtained a search warrant before raiding the compound, they determined that, because of the group's powerful religious beliefs, Koresh and other leaders could harm the other members. To get around this, they attempted a surprise assault. The FBI used flash-bang grenades and loud music to try to get the Davidians to surrender. In April, tanks were used to break down the walls of the complex, and agents pumped in tear gas. A fire then started, and the building burned down in less than an hour. Some reports claim that the Davidians caused the fire; some say that the Davidians were shooting each other in assisted suicide. However, historians believe the FBI caused the fire. Some people, including McVeigh, were upset by the story, believing the FBI had overstepped its authority and violated the rights of the Branch Davidians.

charge, not knowing that he was the perpetrator of that morning's lethal bombing. McVeigh later claimed he thought about shooting the officer, but decided against it since he did not particularly care if he was caught.

At the explosion site, the FBI found the vehicle identification number on the remains of the truck carrying the explosive charge. It was rented to Robert Kling, and a sketch was made from the descriptions of those who worked at the rental business. Soon after, a hotel manager recognized the drawing as McVeigh, and the FBI discovered that he had already been taken into custody by the state trooper. Investigators quickly learned about McVeigh's anti-government feelings and his obsession with the 1993 Branch Davidian incident. They also discovered his links to his friend Nichols, who had helped McVeigh obtain the supplies for the bomb.

A Blasted Aftermath

Nichols refused to talk to the FBI, but a mutual friend, Fortier, told them all they needed to know. McVeigh was indicted on a series of federal counts, including use of a weapon of mass destruction. Both of his court-appointed lawyers had to ask to be relieved of their assignments because

Pictured here, the Alfred P. Murrah Federal Building was destroyed in the blast; the site was later torn down and made into a park.

McVeigh and Oklahoma

A truly remorseless terrorist, McVeigh was not sorry about the number, or ages, of the people his explosion killed. During his trial, he made a statement to those who were affected by his violent actions:

> Death and loss are an integral part of life everywhere. We have to accept it and move on. To those people in Oklahoma who have lost a loved one, I'm sorry, but it happens every day. You're not the first mother to lose a kid, or the first grandparent to lose a grandson or granddaughter. It happens every day, somewhere in the world. I'm not going to go into that courtroom, curl into a fetal ball, and cry just because the victims want me to do that.[1]

1. Quoted in Lou Michel and Dan Herbeck, *American Terrorist: Timothy McVeigh and the Oklahoma City Bombing*. New York, NY: HarperCollins, 2002. PDF e-book.

they had known people killed in the bombing. His new lawyers tried to argue that different terrorists were responsible for the bombing, but McVeigh wanted to take the credit.

The trial lasted for just more than a month, beginning in April 1997, as Fortier testified against McVeigh—although the prosecution had plenty of their own evidence. In addition to McVeigh's excitement over his crimes, there was physical and circumstantial evidence that strongly linked him to the explosion. McVeigh never doubted that he would be found guilty and sentenced to death; he had become the most hated man in America overnight. Most witnesses were those who had lost loved ones in the bombing.

In June, McVeigh was found guilty of 15 counts of murder and conspiracy to commit murder; in August, he was sentenced to death by lethal injection. He was seemingly unfazed by this sentence, asking the court to stop any appeals of his conviction and set the date for his execution. In 2012, after avoiding the death penalty in federal court, Nichols was convicted of 161 counts of murder and sentenced to 161 consecutive life sentences in a super-maximum security prison.

McVeigh did not let his conviction and sentence silence his anti-government philosophies. In fact, he used his newfound celebrity to communicate these thoughts more widely. He did, however, acknowledge that some Americans who might have agreed with his beliefs were horrified by the deaths of innocent children. He defended his actions, pointing out that Americans had prejudiced views about child safety: "It was family convenience that explained the presence of a day-care center placed between street level and the law enforcement agencies … Yet when discussion shifts to Iraq, any day-care center in a government building instantly becomes 'a shield.' Think about that."[22] He wrote a lot while waiting for his execution, including a comparison of how the U.S. military bombs foreign targets to his bombing of a government building. He argued that his act, even if mainstream society disapproved of it, could be justified because he believed the government had acted worse. The only thing he regretted was not completely destroying the building.

McVeigh and Nichols were both associated with the patriot movement, which is made up of political conservatives who reject the authority of the government and law enforcement agencies. It is particularly hard for the government to fight these feelings or prove the violence that results is wrong. This anti-government movement has grown since McVeigh's bombing in 1995. In 2016, the Southern Poverty Law Center identified nearly 1,000 active anti-government groups. These groups are not necessarily violent, but some have committed violent acts that fall into the category of terrorism.

Bombings in Atlanta

One year after the Oklahoma City bombing, Eric Robert Rudolph placed a 40-pound (18.1 kg) bomb filled with nails and screws in Centennial Olympic Park in Atlanta, Georgia, on July 27, 1996. Two people were killed in this bombing: one by the actual explosion and another of a heart attack when he ran to film the scene. About 100 others were injured.

The 1996 Olympics had tight security, with law enforcement patrolling constantly. Rudolph's success shows how difficult it was—and is—to predict and prevent the violent acts of a terrorist. On the day of the bombing, security guard Richard Jewell noticed a suspicious green backpack and alerted the Georgia Bureau of Investigation. Officer Tom Davis was patrolling the area, and he alerted the bomb squad and cleared people from the scene. If Davis had not done this, more people would have been killed.

The FBI immediately made assumptions about the bomber. A popular theory was that he was a white American who planted the bomb so that he could rescue people from it and look like a hero. During the 1984 Olympics, a police officer had claimed to find a bomb before it exploded, but it turned out that he had placed it there himself. This caused many investigators to accuse the security guard, Jewell, who had to spend months convincing the FBI that he was innocent. The FBI followed Jewell around until he hired a lawyer and received $500,000 from lawsuits against the media, which he

In bombing Centennial Olympic Park, Eric Rudolph wanted to make a statement. Like many terror attacks, his bombing had deadly consequences.

claimed were defaming his character. During this time, the real bomber went undetected.

In 1997, there were bombings outside an abortion clinic and a gay nightclub in Atlanta. Shortly afterward, an anonymous letter was sent to newspapers that claimed "abortion and homosexuality were destroying America and [the bomber] was doing what was necessary to save the country from these [evil] forces."[23] This made it clear to investigators that these bombings were not the work of a wannabe hero but of someone looking to send a political message. When a third bombing happened at an abortion clinic in Alabama in 1998, a witness wrote down the license plate of the man fleeing the scene—which led police to Eric Rudolph.

Rudolph's family had instilled anti-government feelings in him from an early age. His mother would travel to Washington, D.C., to protest the use of nuclear weapons and a family friend, Thomas Branham, boasted that he recognized no legal authority. As a child, Rudolph told classmates the Holocaust never happened and that he hated having his photograph taken because he did not want the government to use it to identify him.

Rudolph enlisted in the U.S. Army in 1987, despite his hatred for the government. It was during his time in the military that he learned how to create explosives. After two years, he was discharged for marijuana use. Those who casually knew him described him as becoming more bitter and secretive as time went on. Right before the Olympic bombing, Rudolph was living off the grid and avoiding contact with friends and family.

Finding a Terrorist

Atlanta's Centennial Olympic Park, the site of Rudolph's bombing, was the central area for both athletes and spectators during the 1996 Summer Olympics. The morning of the explosion, up to 100,000 visitors were in that area—luckily, only 110 were injured. Of the two people killed, only one was killed by the bomb: Alice Hawthorne, who had taken her daughter to an Olympic basketball game for her birthday and was posing for a photo when the bomb went off.

Because this bomb succeeded in killing and injuring people despite the millions of dollars spent on security and the thousands of hours spent training individuals to prevent terrorism, investigators felt a heavy pressure to capture the person responsible as soon as possible. The director of the FBI, Louis Freeh, a former federal prosecutor, publicly stated that he was very angry. There were security cameras in the park, but they did not work well because no one had supplied the money to buy tapes that would record high-quality footage.

After the FBI realized that Jewell was not the bomber, there was no clear suspect. Investigators offered a $500,000 reward for information on who the real bomber might be. When Rudolph's next bomb went off in January 1997 at an abortion clinic, it was not immediately

Rudolph's Reasons

Rudolph chose the Olympics because of how much press it received and how bad the bombings would make the FBI and other government organizations look. His later bombings, however, were religiously motivated. His bombing of the abortion clinic relayed his belief that "Abortion is murder. And when the regime in Washington legalized, sanctioned and legitimized this practice, they forfeited their legitimacy and moral authority to govern."[1] He later claimed he bombed the gay nightclub because he felt it legitimized what he felt was "bad behavior." He thought that homosexuality needed to be kept private: "[The] attempt to force society to accept and recognize this behavior [should be met with] force if necessary."[2]

1. Eric Rudolph, "Full Text of Eric Rudolph's Confession," NPR, April 14, 2005. www.npr.org/templates/story/story.php?storyId=4600480.

2. Rudolph, "Full Text of Eric Rudolph's Confession."

---

connected to the Olympic bombing because the bombs were not similarly constructed. After his bomb at a gay night club went off, another bomb was found intact outside of the club—and in it, the investigators found a metal plate that was similar to the previous explosives, giving them their first clue that these attacks were linked.

Soon after, Rudolph sent letters to the press, describing the bombs in detail and saying they were carried out by the Army of God, an anti-abortion extremist organization. However, because the Army of God was not known to use explosives and the fact that Rudolph also referenced the Waco Branch Davidian incident, the FBI grew suspicious that the bombings were done by one person. They went public with this theory and asked the general public to call in if they had any information—but no one did.

Almost a year after the letter, another bomb was placed at a women's health clinic in Birmingham. Here, a witness, Jermaine Jerome Hughes, saw Rudolph running away from the scene. Hughes chased him and called 911. A second citizen took notice and helped, seeing Rudolph get into a car with North Carolina license plates.

Once they had a name, the FBI was able to trace a storage unit that Rudolph had rented, which confirmed that he was responsible for the bombings. The description of Rudolph was then made public information by the United States attorney for northern Alabama, but Rudolph had disappeared—and stayed hidden for the next five years. He was even featured on *America's Most Wanted*, a popular television program that sometimes helped bring in new information, but no good tips were generated. It was taking so long for the FBI to find him that mocking slogans, such as "Eric Rudolph: Hide and Seek Champion 1998"[24] were printed on T-shirts.

Finally, in May 2003, two police officers stopped a man who they thought might be a burglar. Despite the man claiming to be homeless, one of the officers recognized him as Rudolph. Rudolph claimed to be relieved to finally be found. Remorseless for his crimes, he joked with the police officers and offered to autograph wanted posters with his face.

Rudolph pled guilty to the bombings in order to avoid the death penalty. He admitted to bombing the Olympics because they were "under the protection and auspices of the regime in Washington" and were designed "to celebrate the ideals of global socialism."[25] He also said "the purpose of the attack on July 27 was to confound, anger and embarrass the Washington government in the eyes of the world for its [disgusting support] of abortion on demand."[26] Rudolph succeeded in embarrassing the FBI by evading capture for several years. He had initially hoped to knock out Atlanta's power with the bomb and shut down the Olympics—he insisted his intentions were not to hurt innocent people. Nonetheless, he is serving his sentence in a Colorado super-maximum security federal prison.

Chapter Four

AL-QAEDA AND THE WORLD TRADE CENTER ATTACKS

The United States has suffered from many acts of domestic terror, but apart from the Oklahoma City bombing of 1995, the death counts have generally been low. Around the turn of the 21st century, however, international terrorists began importing violence to America. Two separate attacks—in 1993 and 2001—on the World Trade Center in New York City were orchestrated by an Afghanistan-based terror group named al-Qaeda. The latter of these attacks is one of the worst tragedies to ever take place on American soil.

Osama bin Laden

Three years before Eric Rudolph bombed the Atlanta Olympics, a new chapter of American-based terrorism was opening. In 1993, a small group of people who came from halfway around the world—Afghanistan in the Middle East—bombed the World Trade Center in New York City.

One leader organized this group of people: Osama bin Laden.

Bin Laden was born in Riyadh, Saudi Arabia, in March 1957 to a billionaire father. He was the seventh child of 57 and inherited around $30 million after his father's death in 1967. He was raised a Wahhabi Muslim, which is a fundamentalist, militant branch of Islam that teaches there was a perfect age long ago, and Wahhabis need to shape the planet in a way that will recreate and recover that age. This sect of Islam can also be extremist. Bin Laden, in turn, took the most radical approach to Islam and began to hate the Western world from a young age. He believed the "perfect" ancient Muslim world was being corrupted by the influence of Western countries, including the United States. His brand of Wahhibism aimed to fight back against Western civilization and Christian missionaries, whom he believed were a threat to Islam.

Osama bin Laden believed Islam was being corrupted by Western countries—especially the United States.

Al-Qaeda and the World Trade Center Attacks 57

Hoping to spread his extreme ideals, bin Laden arrived in Afghanistan in 1979 to help fight against the Soviet Union, which had invaded the country. The Soviet Union was trying to force Afghanistan to convert to Communism, and the war between the countries lasted 10 years. To support the Afghani Muslim troops (originally called **mujahideen**, Arabic for "those who do jihad"), bin Laden helped bring money into the country. He funded guerrilla combat training and recruited soldiers from religious schools and mosques to fight in the war against Islam. All the while, he was making a name for himself as a powerful Islamic extremist leader who was unafraid of Western powers. Though he did not see much combat action, he was widely regarded as a war hero.

The United States was sending money to Afghanistan through the Pakistani military to help the rebels fight the Soviets. This enabled bin Laden to save some of his personal funds for a future conflict. When the Soviets finally left Afghanistan, bin Laden established a group of mujahideen and other fighters who shared his hatred for Western countries and named it al-Qaeda. Arabic for "the Base," it was originally created so that bin Laden would have information on all his soldiers. The uneasy political situation in Afghanistan, however, made it the perfect country for training jihadists. As al-Qaeda expanded throughout the 1980s and 1990s, bin Laden grew increasingly angry at the United States for its political operations with Russia and in the Middle East.

First World Trade Center Attack

On February 26, 1993, just after noon, a bomb was left in a van in the parking garage beneath the World Trade Center in downtown New York. When it exploded, it created a 100-foot (30 m) wide crater. Six people were killed, and more than 1,000 were injured. Smoke and fire filled the building, which trapped some people inside. It took more than 10 hours to completely evacuate the 50,000 people from the 2 buildings. Four of the six people killed worked for the World Trade Center or the Port Authority—they were having lunch in their basement offices next to the parking garage. The other two victims were an employee of the World Trade Center's restaurant, who was checking on food deliveries in the basement, and a salesman parking his car.

The homemade bomb weighed 1,500 pounds (680 kg) and was made of urea-nitrate. The hole that it tore damaged the support beams badly, and repairing the World Trade Center cost more than $500 million. Investigators were able to uncover the vehicle identification number from the van, which led them to the terrorists responsible. When Mohammad Salameh showed up to collect his security deposit on the rented van, the FBI was waiting for him.

The FBI had been tracking Islamic extremists for months before the bombing occurred. Salameh's arrest led to the arrests of Nidal Ayyad, Mahoud Abouhalima, and Ahmed Ajaj. The mastermind behind the bombing, however,

Before the September 11 attacks, the Twin Towers were among the most iconic buildings in the world.

Additional Bombers

The sixth man responsible for the 1993 terrorist plot was Eyad Ismoil, who drove the van that held the bomb. He was not convicted until April 1998, after being arrested in Jordan in 1995. He was a Jordanian citizen born in Kuwait. He came to the United States in 1989 to study engineering at Wichita State University. Ismoil was 21 at the time of the bombing. He helped Yousef load the bomb into the van and light the fuse. Before his sentencing, he claimed that not everyone who is convicted of crimes is guilty—his lawyers had tried to argue that Ismoil did not know there was a bomb in the van but thought it was a shipment of cleaning products. Ismoil was ordered to pay more than $10 million in restitution. There is a seventh man believed to be responsible for the bombing, Abdul Rahman Yasin, who has never been apprehended. In 2005, the U.S. Department of State offered a $5 million reward for any information leading to his capture.

was Ramzi Yousef, who had coordinated the attack under the orders of bin Laden and had intended for the bomb to knock down one of the towers, causing it to collapse onto the other. He claimed to have chosen the World Trade Center buildings because they were among the most recognizable symbols of America. He had intentions of additional attacks on other New York landmarks, such as the United Nations and the FBI offices, but he fled the country the night of the 1993 bombing. Salameh and Yousef had ties to the Farouq mosque in Brooklyn, which was associated with Omar Abdel-Rahman, who had influenced bin Laden. Yousef was the nephew of Khalid Shaikh Mohammed, the man later accused of planning the 2001 attacks on the World Trade Center and the Pentagon, which killed almost 3,000 people.

A Conclusion?

Salameh, Ayyad, Abouhalima, and Ajaj were convicted in 1994 for their involvement in the bombing, and each was sentenced to 240 years in prison. Yousef, however, was not arrested until 1996, when he was found in Pakistan planning to bomb U.S. planes in Asia. Before he was sentenced, Yousef gave a statement saying, in part, "Yes, I am a terrorist, and proud of it as long as it is against the U.S. government," which he accused of being "more than terrorists; you are the one who invented terrorism … You are butchers, liars and hypocrites."²⁷ He was sentenced to life in prison, plus 240 years. In addition to this jail term, a judge fined Yousef $4.5 million and ordered him to pay $250 million in restitution. Though he did not have nearly enough money to pay this, such a steep fine meant that any money he might make from a book or movie about his life would go to his victims. The judge described Yousef as "a virus that must be locked away."²⁸ He was placed in solitary confinement at a super-maximum security Colorado prison. He is permitted to read books and watch television, but newspapers and magazines are censored to prevent him from receiving messages from the outside world.

Relative to earlier incidents of domestic terror, New York police and the FBI found and apprehended those responsible with speed and ease. After the second attack on the World Trade Center, in 2001, this would prove to have negative effects. The 9/11 Commission Report, the official document that reported the events that led up to the attacks, claimed the speed and

The 1993 World Trade Center bombing resulted in six deaths, thousands of injuries, and hundreds of millions of dollars in damages.

Al-Qaeda and the World Trade Center Attacks **61**

efficiency that resolved the 1993 bombing were unfortunate because "it created an impression that the law enforcement system was well-equipped to cope with terrorism."[29] Because the 1993 bombing was resolved so quickly, few investigators thought to look into reasons for the attack. This grave error prevented the realization that there were threats of future terrorist activity—including the September 11 attacks.

Counterterrorism

In 1986, the Central Intelligence Agency (CIA) established the Counterterrorism Center (CTC) as a division of the National Clandestine Service. The director is anonymous for security reasons and uses the code name "Roger." It was established because the evolving threat of terrorism ignored geographic boundaries, and an organization was needed that could go beyond those boundaries to fight terrorism.

By the early 1990s, the CTC was understaffed. Roughly 100 employees were split into branches that dealt with different international issues, such as the Japanese Red Army or Islamic radicalism in Algeria. The attacks on the World Trade Center in 1993, however, proved that terrorism had taken a new face and came with a whole new set of obstacles. The major threat was now coming from the Middle East. In January 1996, three years after the first World Trade Center attack, the CTC opened the Bin Laden Issue Station to track bin Laden and al-Qaeda. In the late 1990s, Counterterrorist Intelligence Centers were established to collaborate with other countries' intelligence agencies to keep track of Islamist extremists. After the terrorist attack in 2001, these centers expanded rapidly.

Bin Laden and "the Plan"

The United States first heard of bin Laden when they found his phone number on the list of calls made by Yousef after the 1993 World Trade Center bombing. A CIA paper in 1993 described bin Laden as "an independent actor [who] sometimes works with other individuals and governments"[30] in support of extremist Islam. That same year, the CTC started monitoring bin Laden's activities—something they rarely did to individuals.

In August 1996, bin Laden issued the Declaration of Jihad on the Americans Occupying the Country of the Two Holiest Sites, meaning al-Qaeda was now officially at war with the United States, whether the United States was fully aware of this or not. The federal government did not pay much attention to bin Laden at the time, instead being distracted by other figures, such as Saddam Hussein, leader of a growing Iraqi threat. In February 1998, bin Laden formed the World Islamic Front for Jihad Against Jews and Crusaders, which claimed that the duty of every Muslim in every country was to kill all the Americans and their allies—civilian and military.

The overwhelming majority of Muslims ignored this decree, but some extremists sided with bin Laden. In August 1998, a suicide bomber killed 12 Americans and

A Boating Incident

In 2000, bin Laden attacked the USS *Cole*, a U.S. Navy guided-missile destroyer, in Yemen. A much smaller boat, loaded with explosives, was sent by bin Laden. It ripped a massive hole in the side of the destroyer, killing 17 sailors and injuring around 40. After this attack, bin Laden prepared for what he thought would be a violent retaliation by the United States—but the government did not strike back. This made him more aggressive and bold. The United States discussed the incident with the government of Yemen but found that they needed credible sources and proof that the attack came from al-Qaeda.

more than 200 others at the U.S. Embassy in Nairobi, Kenya. In response to this violence, bin Laden said, "When it becomes apparent that it would be impossible to repeal these Americans without assaulting them, even as this involved the killing of Muslims, this is permissible under Islam … Let history be a witness that I am a criminal."[31] That December, the chief of the CIA declared war on bin Laden. In 1999, he ordered a new plan of attack be drawn up against al-Qaeda. This became known as "the Plan" and was described to the National Security Agency (NSA), the FBI, and other government intelligence agencies. With this strategy, a specialized cell of officers was formed. They would meet daily to discuss how to fight bin Laden, al-Qaeda, and their vision for a world of Muslim radicalism.

The United States had learned that bin Laden would be at a meeting at a camp in Afghanistan, so they began Operation Infinite Reach, launching more than 70 missiles at the camp. Bin Laden escaped this attack, which made him an even bigger celebrity to his followers. By September 1999, the CTC had learned that bin Laden was planning a major terrorist attack on the United States in the near future. They identified and conducted surveillance on at least one man involved in the 2001 attacks, but this did not prevent the violent terrorism to come.

Forming a Terrorist Team

The CTC's intelligence was accurate—bin Laden was planning a huge terrorist attack against the United States. He gathered a team of suicide terrorists from four different countries: Egypt, the United Arab Emirates, Lebanon, and Yemen. These four men would be the major players in the September 11 attacks. Mohammed Atta, from Egypt, learned about the plan to use airplanes as weapons in 1999. It appealed to him because it did not involve smuggling bombs—the planes would cause the destruction. They did not have to come up with a complicated escape plan because there would be no escape.

In March 2000, Atta sent an e-mail about attending a flight school in Florida, asking if he and a group of other Arabs could enroll. Reports also indicate he sent similar messages to dozens of other flight programs across America, hoping to get a response. He came to the United States in June 2000 and earned a pilot's license in September. Ziad Jarrah also earned his license in Florida. Khalid al-Mihdhar and Nawaf al-Hazmi attended flight school in California, but both flunked out. Atta was given a message from al-Qaeda in July 2001; bin Laden was anxious to put the plan into action because so many men with terrorist connections living in America at the same time would eventually get the attention of the government.

September 11, 2001

In August, the four men bought their tickets for flights on the morning of September 11. That day, Atta flew from Portland, Maine, to Boston, Massachusetts at 6 a.m. without any problem. He was selected for additional screening by security, but that just meant making sure he boarded the plane before his luggage was loaded. Once in Boston, he boarded American Airlines Flight 11 for Los Angeles at around 8 a.m. On the plane were 2 pilots, 9 flight attendants, and 81 passengers—among them were 5 terrorists.

Reports indicate that the plane was hijacked by Atta within 15 minutes of takeoff. Two flight attendants made emergency calls saying that two other attendants had been stabbed and the cockpit was not answering. At 8:46 a.m., the plane collided with the North Tower of the World Trade Center, and everyone onboard was killed instantly.

United Airlines also had an 8 a.m. flight out of Boston to Los Angeles, which carried 2 pilots, 7 flight attendants, and 56 passengers, including 5 terrorists. This flight was also hijacked at knifepoint. A passenger, Peter Hanson, was able to call his father and explain that something terrible was happening—his father immediately called the police. At 9:03 a.m., this plane hit the South Tower of the World Trade Center; no one on the plane survived.

American Airlines Flight 77 left Washington, D.C., that morning at 8:20, carrying 2 pilots, 4 flight attendants, and 58 passengers, with another 5 terrorists on board. At 9:37 a.m., the plane crashed into the Pentagon, killing everyone on impact.

At 8:41 a.m., United Airlines Flight 93 departed Newark, New Jersey, for San Francisco, carrying 2 pilots, 5 flight attendants, and 37 passengers, including 4 terrorists. The flight was supposed to take off at 8 a.m. sharp, but it was delayed for 42 minutes; this made a big difference in the result of the attack. Just after 9 a.m., the pilots received a warning that said:

"Beware any cockpit intrusion—Two a/c [aircraft] hit World Trade Center."³² When the terrorists began their attack on this plane, the passengers started calling loved ones at home. These calls made the passengers and crew aware of the fates of the other hijacked planes, and they knew there was reason to panic.

It is believed United 93 was headed for the U.S. Capitol Building or the White House. However, passengers took the initiative and rushed the terrorists as they tried to take over, forcing them to crash in an empty field in Pennsylvania just after 10 a.m., killing everyone onboard. This action undoubtedly saved hundreds of additional lives.

The scene at the World Trade Center's Twin Towers was horrific. Survivors rushed to get out of the buildings. The South Tower fell first, even though it was the second to be hit. Two hundred people fell or jumped from the buildings and were killed. When the North Tower

The force of the planes flying into the Twin Towers completely destroyed both buildings and parts of the surrounding area.

fell, the chief of the Fire Department of New York, the Port Authority Police Department superintendent, and other senior law enforcement and emergency response personnel were killed. At the Pentagon, 70 civilians and 55 military personnel were killed when the plane hit the building. Nearly 3,000 people were killed in the September 11 attacks—more than 2,700 in New York alone, making it the largest terrorist attack in the history of the world to date.

Afterward

In the wake of the destruction, the September 11th Victim Compensation Fund was created. This organization processes requests for money to pay for deaths,

On any other day, an attack on the Pentagon would have been the main focus of international news for weeks, but the devastation in New York was far greater.

> ## Pennsylvania Eyewitness
>
> In the Pennsylvanian field where United 93 crashed, no one on the ground was killed. It seems like a miracle that the plane avoided crashing into a residential or commercial area—especially since the hijackers were trying to cause as many deaths as possible. There was, however, an eyewitness who saw the plane pass by overheard: "It was low enough I thought you could probably count the rivets. You could see more of the roof of the plane than you could the belly. It was on its side. There was a great explosion and you could see the flames."[1]
>
> 1. Quoted in J. Michael Martinez, *Terrorist Attacks on American Soil: From the Civil War Era to the Present*. Plymouth, UK: Rowman & Littlefield, 2012, p. 393.

medical bills, and other expenses incurred by victims of the attacks. As of 2016, it has paid more than $1.5 billion to victims and family members. The economic loss in the weeks after the attack was estimated at more than $100 billion. It took millions of hours of labor and $750 million to clean up 1.8 million tons (1.6 million mt) of debris from the fall of the Twin Towers. The total cleanup effort took more than a year.

Americans and the U.S. government would never think of terrorism in the same way after the attacks on September 11. The damage and number of lives lost were unimaginable. No one had any doubt that al-Qaeda and bin Laden were responsible. This day highlighted how unprepared America was for an attack of this magnitude. The CTC knew an attack on U.S. soil was a possibility, but they did not completely understand the capability of foreign terrorists to destroy domestic targets. Because of this weakness in security, the Department of Homeland Security (DHS) was created as a department of the federal government with a mission of antiterrorism and disaster prevention.

The Department of Homeland Security officially opened March 1, 2003, with the mandate to oversee and coordinate "a comprehensive national strategy to safeguard the country against terrorism and respond to any future attacks."[33] It is divided into four components: Border and Transportation Security; Emergency Preparedness and Response; Chemical, Biological, Radiological and Nuclear Countermeasures; and Information Analysis and Infrastructure Protection. Its seal was designed to portray images of land, sea, and air to communicate that the department would prevent and protect the United States against terrorism from anywhere. The eagle's wings extend past the circle of the symbol to indicate that the Department of Homeland Security would perform its functions differently than traditional administrations had in the past.

Although the country had been devastated by the attack, the authorities had to act quickly to bring justice and send a message to bin Laden and other Muslim radicals that the United States would not tolerate terrorism. The government went after bin Laden, but it proved difficult to locate him. In December 2001, a video

The creation of the Department of Homeland Security was a direct response to the September 11 attacks.

> ## Obama Addresses the Nation
>
> After bin Laden was killed, Obama gave a speech about the mission to the country. He did not celebrate the death, but instead emphasized how the world was safer without bin Laden in it:
>
> *The cause of securing our country is not complete. But tonight, we are once again reminded that America can do whatever we set our mind to. That is the story of our history, whether it's the pursuit of prosperity for our people, or the struggle for equality for all our citizens; our commitment to stand up for our values abroad, and our sacrifices to make the world a safer place.*[1]
>
> 1. Barack Obama, "Osama Bin Laden Dead," White House, May 2, 2011. obamawhitehouse.archives.gov/blog/2011/05/02/osama-bin-laden-dead.

surfaced that showed bin Laden was alive and intended to continue fighting against the West. Years passed without proof of his whereabouts. Nearly a decade after the largest terrorist attack in history, intelligence informed President Barack Obama that bin Laden had been located in Pakistan. On May 1, 2011, Navy SEALs flew into Pakistan and assassinated bin Laden while Obama oversaw the operation from the White House.

Chapter Five

TERRORISM AFTER SEPTEMBER 11

From the federal government to local law enforcement to everyday life for millions of Americans, things have changed dramatically since the September 11 attacks. Air travel security has been tightened, new prevention policies have been implemented, and people are on the lookout for any sign of a terrorist attack. In many ways, the destruction of the World Trade Center was the "perfect" act of terrorism: Not only did it claim the lives of thousands of innocents, it also left hundreds of millions in fear of when the next attack would come.

Life After Destruction

In 2002, the Pew Research Center polled Americans on how safe they felt. Researchers asked Americans how effective they believed the changed, and supposedly improved, security regulations put in place by the government would be in stopping future terrorist attacks: 39 percent said nothing had changed since the attacks, 33 percent said the country's defenses had gotten better, and 22 percent said the United States was less safe than before September 11. In 2016, 40 percent of Americans polled thought the country was more susceptible to terrorism than it was in 2001. This was less because of America's security measures and more because of the growing strength of extremist groups. Accordingly, only 25 percent of Americans believed terrorists were less capable of carrying out a similar attack.

Along with the creation of the Department of Homeland Security, the USA PATRIOT Act was instated in 2001. The name stands for Uniting and Strengthening America by Providing Appropriate Tools Required to Intercept and Obstruct Terrorism. The act expanded the surveillance powers of federal law enforcement and intelligence agencies. This meant the government was allowed to search out, eavesdrop on, and record communications that might be threatening to the United States and its citizens. The act allowed the FBI to undertake surveillance operations on U.S. citizens without substantial proof that they were involved in terrorist activity. Despite this, acts of terrorism would continue into the 21st century.

Fort Hood Shootings

On November 5, 2009, Major Nidal Malik Hasan, a psychiatrist for the U.S. Army, killed 13 people and injured 32 in a mass shooting at Fort Hood military base in Texas. Hasan, born in the United States to Palestinian parents, turned from peaceful to radical Islam sometime after the September 11 attacks. He was scheduled to deploy to Afghanistan, but he did not want to fight other Muslims. He believed "he had a jihad duty to kill as many [American] soldiers as possible."[34]

The day of the shooting, Hasan brought two handguns—wrapped in paper towels to muffle the sound—and hundreds of rounds of ammunition. When he opened fire, he was shot and paralyzed by the return fire. For his court-martial (a criminal trial of a member of the armed forces), Hasan chose to represent himself. In his opening statement, he said, "We mujahedeen are trying to establish the perfect religion … I apologize for the mistakes I made in this endeavor."[35] He did not call witnesses or present evidence to prove why he should not be sentenced to death for his actions. When he was convicted of the 13 murders and 32 counts of attempted murder, the death penalty was recommended. As the jury announced this verdict, Hasan was emotionless and silent.

Hasan claimed he was willing to die as a martyr for Islam; he believed he was fighting for his radical ideals when he carried out the shooting. The Internet history on his computer included many key terms and alarming searches about suicide bombings, mass shootings, and how murder fits into the Muslim faith. Investigators found that he had been communicating via email with radicals across the globe. Hasan is an example of the modern wave of lone-wolf terrorism. September 11 was the last major attack carried out by a group of terrorists on American soil. The attacks that have happened since then, including Hasan's, have been carried out by individuals who find themselves called to extremist Islam. Though some of these terrorists are in contact with groups such as al-Qaeda, others act on their radical impulses without any organizational support.

Five years after Hasan's attack, another shooting took place at Fort Hood. In April 2014, Ivan Lopez, an Iraq War veteran who showed no symptoms of depression to his peers or superiors, opened fire at the base, killing 3 people and injuring 16 before killing himself. His commanding officers later said the attack was most likely the result of an argument over his requested time off, but Lopez's father suspected his son was not mentally well. Lopez was receiving ongoing treatment

Nidal Hasan felt he had a duty as a radical Muslim to kill as many Americans as possible, following Osama bin Laden's orders.

for his mental health, and his mother and grandfather had died shortly before his shooting took place. It was reported that he was upset by how long it took the military to grant his time off for the funerals.

Lopez complained about having suffered a traumatic brain injury when deployed, but army medical personnel could not identify any specific traumatic event or contact with the enemy in Lopez's combat experiences. He was getting treatment for depression, but was not diagnosed with PTSD. He did, however, have a history of lying, and there was proof he was trying to receive disability payments from the department of Veterans Affairs despite not being medically disabled. His act of violence seemed to stem from his dissatisfaction with the U.S. Army and is not truly considered an act of terror. This is a clear difference from Hasan, who aligned his beliefs specifically with extremist Muslims and acted as a terrorist because of religious radicalism.

The Boston Marathon Bombings

On April 15, 2013, two bombs went off near the finish line of the Boston Marathon, killing three people—a young boy and two women—and injuring hundreds. The bombs were placed near the finish line because that is where the highest concentration of people was going to be; they exploded around 12 seconds apart. They contained pellets and nails that were held in pressure cookers, hidden inside backpacks that had been left there earlier.

Three days after, as federal and local law enforcement tried to find the terrorists, a campus police officer was killed at the Massachusetts Institute of Technology and a car was hijacked in nearby Cambridge, Massachusetts. Police chased the car, and the driver and passenger threw explosives at them. After a lengthy chase and shootout, one of the suspects died from bullet wounds, but the other fled and went into hiding. The bombers were identified as 26-year-old Tamerlan Tsarnaev and 19-year-old Dzhokhar Tsarnaev—brothers living in Cambridge after having legally immigrated from Chechnya. Dzhokhar was a student at the University of Massachusetts–Dartmouth.

It is still unclear if Dzhokhar Tsarnaev bombed Boston because of extremist Islamic beliefs.

The bombing of the Boston Marathon killed three people.

The day after the car chase, Dzhokhar was found in a boat parked in a driveway, hiding and badly injured.

Dzhokhar Tsarnaev was charged with using a weapon of mass destruction that resulted in death. He pled not guilty to 30 charges related to the attacks, but in 2015, he was found guilty of all charges and sentenced to death. He was ordered to pay more than $100 million in restitution to the victims. After sentencing, he apologized and admitted his guilt to the court. As of 2017, he was held at a super-maximum security prison in Colorado. His brother was buried in a cemetery in Virginia after three cemeteries in Massachusetts refused the body.

It is still unclear whether these brothers meant to send a message of Muslim extremism as jihadists or whether they simply wanted to kill as many people as possible. Regardless, this was an undoubted act of terrorism that killed innocent people and scared citizens across the country. At the time of the car chase and manhunt, thousands of police officers were in the area—some showing up without the orders to do so. Because so many law enforcement agents were present, the suspect was identified and caught quickly, which prevented further chaos and loss of life.

Chattanooga Shooting

On July 16, 2015, Mohammad Youssuf Abdulazeez shot seven people and killed five at the Navy Operations Support Center in Chattanooga, Tennessee. Four of those killed were Marines, and the fifth was a U.S. Navy sailor. Abdulazeez had three guns on him, but only two were legally obtained.

Abdulazeez was a well-liked electrical engineering graduate of the University of Tennessee. He owned several guns legally and went to shooting ranges as a hobby. A friend insisted that before the attack he was "the coolest guy [who] was always so positive about people … Whatever caused this to happen, it's not him, it's not normal. That's not how he is."[36] Abdulazeez was born in Kuwait in 1990, but he was naturalized as a citizen of the United States. His former classmates described him as a somewhat devout Muslim who would often pray—but would also sometimes skip Islamic traditions. He had been in Jordan, a country close to Iraq, Afghanistan, and Syria, where many extremist Muslims hide, as recently as 2014 visiting family. His friend claimed that after Abdulazeez spent some time in Jordan, he seemed like a different person: "Something happened over there … I'm sure he had something that happened to him overseas."[37]

Abdulazeez was not in any U.S. database of suspected terrorists, nor did he have a history of violence. After the shooting, the FBI director at the time, James Comey, said, "There is no doubt that the Chattanooga killer was inspired, motivated by foreign terrorist organization propaganda."[38] Comey could not, however, determine which terrorist group had inspired Abdulazeez. In response to the shootings, some governors have increased security at National Guard

Former FBI director James Comey was quick to draw attention to the fact that Abdulazeez may have been influenced by foreign terrorist organizations.

recruiting stations; in Texas, recruiting agents are armed in case of an attack. President Obama also weighed in on the shooting:

> [American] intelligence and law enforcement agencies have disrupted countless plots here and overseas ... our military and counterterrorism professionals have relentlessly pursued terrorist networks overseas ... Over the last few years, however, the terrorist threat has evolved into a new phase. As we've become better at preventing complex, multifaceted attacks like 9/11, terrorists turned to less complicated acts of violence like the mass shootings that are all too common in our society. It is this type of attack that we saw at Fort Hood in 2009; in Chattanooga earlier this year.[39]

San Bernardino

In December 2015, a man and woman opened fire at a holiday party in San Bernardino, California, killing 14 people and injuring 21. The party was at the Inland Regional Center, a facility for people with developmental disabilities. The shooters were U.S. citizen Syed Rizwan Farook, 28 years old, and his wife Tashfeen Malik, 29 years old. Farook had angrily left the center that morning and returned at 11 a.m. with Malik—both were dressed in tactical assault gear that held ammunition. They opened fire and then fled the scene in a rented SUV. Police traced them to their apartment, where an SUV matching the description of the getaway vehicle passed by. Law enforcement pursued it. After leading police on a chase, Farook and Malik were killed in a shootout with the officers.

Before the attack, Farook had been a county health inspector for five years. He graduated from California State University in 2010 with a degree in environmental health. He had a six-month-old daughter with Malik, who was in the United States on a special visa from Pakistan because she was engaged to Farook. Investigators found that Farook had been in touch with more than one person who was being investigated by the FBI as a possible international terrorist. He had been to Pakistan and Saudi Arabia in 2013 for the Hajj—the annual Islamic pilgrimage to Mecca, the most holy city for Muslims—and this is where he met Malik.

The guns that Farook and Malik used were purchased legally. They were known to practice at shooting ranges before the attack. They left a bag of explosives at the holiday party that were rigged to a remote-controlled car. The police also found 12 pipe bombs and hundreds of bomb-making tools at their apartment. Investigators believed that Farook might have planned an earlier attack with someone else in 2012 but did not go through with it.

Malik's final Facebook post pledged allegiance to ISIS, the dangerous terrorist organization based in Syria that carries on bin Laden's extremist message. Investigators believed that Malik was radicalized

Syed Rizwan Farook (right) was a U.S. citizen who became an extremist. He and Tashfeen Malik were killed after murdering 14 people in San Bernardino.

by ISIS before she came to the United States and might have pushed her husband into committing the terrorist attack, but it is possible that the husband and wife planned the attack entirely on their own, without any instruction from a larger terrorist organization. As President Obama mentioned in his address following the Chattanooga shooting, instances of lone-wolf terrorism are becoming the standard tactic of ISIS, al-Qaeda, and supporters of radical causes around the world.

Orlando Nightclub Shooting

On June 12, 2016, Omar Mateen, a 29-year-old security guard, killed 49 people and injured 53 in a shooting at a gay nightclub in Orlando, Florida. After a three-hour standoff, he was shot and killed by police. It was the deadliest shooting by a single shooter in U.S. history and the deadliest terror attack in the United States since September 11.

Shortly after he started shooting people, Mateen called police on his phone. He called to swear allegiance to ISIS and claim that his act of violence was caused

After Mateen killed 49 people in Orlando, memorials such as this were common sights.

by the assassination of Abu Waheeb—a leader of ISIS—in Iraq the month before. He also said he was shooting people because of America's intervention in Iraq and Syria and that it needed to stop. The CIA investigated Mateen, but found no pre-existing links between him and ISIS.

Mateen was born and raised in New York to Afghan parents. Former coworkers said that, despite his upbringing, he had a lot of hatred for racial minorities, Jewish people, and members of the LGBT+ community. Despite this, regular customers of the club recalled seeing him there as a patron on a dozen occasions. Investigators have speculated that he was there to plan his attack. After the shooting, businesses, especially places that get very busy and crowded, took steps to increase security. Similarly, the Orlando Police Department upgraded the equipment their officers wear to include bulletproof helmets. The day after the shooting, ISIS took responsibility for Mateen's actions and the results, proudly proclaiming him as one of their agents.

Epilogue

BATTLING TERRORISM TODAY

Though America has been targeted by acts of lone-wolf terrorism in the 2010s, many terrorists are based in politically unstable countries in the Middle East—and they are not acting alone. There are many groups, including ISIS, that call war-torn countries, such as Syria and Iraq, their home and plan out attacks from there. The fact that—as of 2017—there has not been another large-scale attack on U.S. soil since 2001 is a testament to the improved security and protection policies of the government.

ISIS

The acts of terrorism that occur in the 21st century, such as the San Bernardino and Orlando shootings, are most often acts that come from followers of the Islamic State, or ISIS. ISIS is a radical Muslim organization that exists with the purpose of reinstating sharia law. Sharia law is a system of morals and rules established for Muslims to follow in order to lead righteous lives, according to certain branches of Islam. ISIS believes that Western countries, especially the United States and most of those in Europe, represent a threat to the morality and ideals of extreme sharia law. ISIS does not tolerate other forms of religion; that is why they take responsibility for attacks all over the world on those who hold different religious or political views.

Although ISIS was not formed when the World Trade Center was attacked, its origins can be traced back to Osama bin Laden. Al-Qaeda's mission was to establish an Islamic state all over the world—not just in Afghanistan or the Middle East. They hated the United States specifically because its government does not follow rules of

The United States has been involved in global antiterrorist efforts for more than 15 years; defense secretary Jim Mattis is shown here in front of a map of the Middle East region.

extremist Islam. The founder of ISIS, Abu Musab al-Zarqawi, was very attracted to the holy war against Western culture that al-Qaeda encouraged. Despite a rocky relationship with bin Laden and an early death, al-Zarqawi was able to establish an ideal that appealed to many Muslims in Iraq: that Islam should be the dominant—and only—religion in the world and all faithful Muslims should be willing to die to achieve this goal.

As of 2017, the leader of ISIS was Abu Bakr al-Baghdadi. He and his extremist followers believe they must follow the example of Muhammad—Islam's founder and first prophet—and that most of the world needs to die. He has preached that a final battle will be fought in Syria when the Muslims will fight against those who oppose Islam. He has also taught that Muslims who wish to go to heaven must fight on the correct side. This has

Abu Bakr al-Baghdadi has proven to be an outgoing and powerful leader of ISIS. He is shown here giving a famous speech after he and ISIS captured a major Iraqi city, Mosul, in 2014.

caused young radical Muslims from all over the world to attempt to travel to Syria and Iraq to join the Islamic State's cause. However, foreign governments have caught on, and it has become increasingly difficult for these extremist Muslims to travel internationally. When these individuals grow increasingly frustrated at not being able to physically join the fight in the Middle East, some have decided to lash out at their home countries in acts of lone-wolf terrorism.

When these acts of terror and violence occur in Europe and America, it is rarely the case that ISIS has trained or sent terrorists with attack orders, as happened in 2001 with al-Qaeda. Instead, many bombings and mass shootings are carried out by extremist terrorists who sympathize with what ISIS teaches. In this way, they are achieving the Islamic State's main objective and spreading fear, resentment, and anger around the world. The leaders of ISIS want the world to hate Muslims because it will prove that the world is an enemy of Islam, which they believe will attract more radical recruits. Because the most prominent modern terrorists come from the Middle East, the world has become increasingly Islamophobic, even though a vast majority of Muslims strongly oppose what ISIS is doing.

How to Fight

Since the threats from ISIS are dangerous, it is clear that the domestic terror threats are very real and serious. They are also hard to predict and prevent. Multiple departments within the U.S. government have been created to deal with the threat of terrorism, both domestic and foreign.

One former counterterrorism expert at the Department of Homeland Security said, "9/11 has set the threshold for what terrorism is in the minds of many Americans, and if domestic terrorism lacks the magnitude, it must not be terrorism."[40] Domestic terrorism, as defined by the FBI, used to be Americans attacking other Americans because of extremist ideas, such as in the cases of Ted Kaczynski and Timothy McVeigh. Now, most acts of domestic terrorism are based on imported extremist ideas and are no less of a threat than foreign-born attacks. Therefore, as a country, the United States must be well equipped and prepared to prevent and fight internal and external potential attacks.

Department of Homeland Security

The Department of Homeland Security is the third largest department of the federal government. It is responsible for:

> *counterterrorism, cybersecurity, aviation security, border security, port security, maritime security, administration and enforcement*

Battling Terrorism Today **85**

of immigration laws, protection of national leaders, protection of critical infrastructure, detection of and protection against chemical, biological and nuclear threats to [America], and response to disasters.[41]

The DHS employs nearly 230,000 people who work among 22 sub-departments, including the Transportation Security Administration (TSA), Secret Service, Customs and Border Protection, Federal Emergency Management Agency (FEMA), Coast Guard, and Immigration Services.

The TSA is responsible for the security of anyone traveling in America. They are mostly involved in regulating security in air travel. Their employees screen passengers at airports, supply armed federal air marshals on planes, and keep bomb-sniffing dogs available. The TSA has made air travel much different after the September 11 attacks. They are responsible for safety and security at more than 450 airports in the United States. Some airports hire private firms to do screenings, but these firms still need to get TSA approval and follow standards.

Customs and Border Protection is the largest law enforcement agency within the DHS. Its duties include preventing terrorists from entering the United States and preventing illegal drugs from being smuggled across the borders.

Immigration Services processes immigrant visa and refugee applications as effectively and quickly as possible. They also help immigrants become citizens through the naturalization process. This includes living in the United States as a law-abiding citizen for five years.

President Jimmy Carter originally created FEMA as its own organization in 1979, but it is now part of the DHS. Its purpose is to coordinate a response to national disasters too large for city or state authorities to handle on their own. In the case of such a situation, the governor declares a state of emergency and directs FEMA to respond to the disaster. They provide evacuation support, assistance to refugees, and rescue efforts.

The Coast Guard is a branch of the U.S. military. During peacetime, it operates under the DHS, but if war is declared, it operates under the authority of Congress. The primary responsibility of the Coast Guard is to maintain safety across American waters.

The Secret Service is a law enforcement agency within the DHS whose most famous responsibility is protecting current and former presidents and vice presidents. However, many Secret Service agents are also tasked with investigating counterfeit currency and major fraud cases.

Central Intelligence Agency

The CIA was formed in 1947 from the Office of Strategic Services. Before its creation, the FBI and the Offices of the Naval and Army Intelligences dealt with intelligence, but this created problems of competition and rivalry and a lack of coordination. As a result of this lack of coordination, President Franklin

The CIA was formed in 1947, and it has become one of the most famous—and infamous—federal agencies.

D. Roosevelt did not receive important information on Japan before they attacked the United States at Pearl Harbor in 1941. The United States was the last of the world superpowers to have an intelligence agency.

The CIA is responsible for gathering and analyzing security information from around the world. It takes this information and provides it to the president. The CIA is not law enforcement like the FBI, and it does not focus heavily on domestic intelligence. It is the only agency authorized to carry out actions on behalf of the president. It was responsible for locating bin Laden and has been focused on counterterrorism. Going forward, the CIA has recognized cyberwarfare as a threat to the security of the country and has made efforts to counter these attacks by using technology offensively.

National Security Agency

The NSA was founded in 1952 by President Harry S. Truman as an agency that would "provide an effective, unified organization and control of the communications intelligence activities of the United States conducted against foreign governments, and to provide for integrated operational policies and procedures pertaining thereto."[42] It operates as part of the Department of Defense. Because it was not created by Congress, it does not fall under the review standards of congressional organizations. The NSA is the most secret intelligence agency in America.

The NSA has the responsibility of keeping communications from the government from being intercepted or manipulated. It also collects information from other countries, sometimes by physically bugging electronic equipment—meaning it can listen in on private conversations.

The NSA is restricted to intercepting international communications, meaning it cannot target private citizens unless they are employed by another country. In 2013, a computer security contractor, Edward Snowden, leaked classified information about two NSA surveillance programs that collected information from Americans via the Internet and cell phone calls. These programs were collecting information and spying on American citizens even though they were not supposed to.

Past and Present

Since the 1857 Mountain Meadows Massacre, terrorism has drastically changed and evolved. Throughout most of American history, terrorism was often seen as one small, domestic group committing violence in order to communicate a message to a larger domestic organization. Through the 1980s and 1990s, the face of terrorism was angry white men, such as Ted Kaczynski and Timothy McVeigh, who felt the government had too much power and would sacrifice lives to send a message. Today, many people think of the religion of Islam when hearing

After leaking classified information, Edward Snowden fled the United States to hide in Russia.

the about a terrorist attack.

Predictably, the way the United States battles terrorism has also evolved. Cases before and during the Civil War were seen as issues of race and were often handled by local law enforcement. Anti-government acts of terrorism called for the involvement of the FBI. At the turn of the 21st century, however, the battle against terrorism became even more serious, and the need for the right weapons to fight terrorism became extremely important. This is where the DHS came in. The government realized that September 11, 2001, revealed a large hole in its antiterrorism efforts—and that finding Ted Kaczynski in a cabin in Montana was easy compared to finding Osama bin Laden in a compound in Pakistan.

Islamophobia

It is difficult to predict how terrorism might further evolve and change from what the world sees now. If terrorism were predictable, battling it would be much easier. Some have tried to stereotype an entire group—Muslims or any Middle Easterner—based on fear. Because ISIS has become a prominent terrorist threat, Muslims in general have been stereotyped as possible terrorists. There exists strong Islamophobia in the United States that is particularly applied to immigrants from the Middle East.

It is important to realize that most Muslims are not extremist radicals and only a small percentage of Islamic believers pose a threat to the United States. Suspecting every Muslim of terrorism or allegiance to ISIS is exactly what the Islamic State wants. The more the West hates Muslims, the more justified ISIS feels when killing Americans or Europeans. For these reasons, many have criticized the travel ban ordered by President Donald Trump in 2017. His executive order was created to restrict travel to the United States from seven mostly Muslim countries: Iraq, Syria, Sudan, Iran, Libya, Yemen, and Somalia. However, opponents have claimed this order is prejudicial and unfair because very few immigrants are actually terrorist threats. As of 2017, the Supreme Court was waiting to hear cases against the ban.

The Future Terrorist

In 2015, the United States prosecuted 60 alleged terrorists—more than in any year since 2001. According to then U.S. Assistant Attorney General John Carlin, almost all of these cases were triggered by ISIS's use of social media to communicate with extremist Muslims in the United States. This means that U.S. citizens were being encouraged—in their own homes—to carry out acts of violence in their communities. There was even a booklet released in early 2015 by ISIS that was a guide on how to secretly blend into a non-Muslim country, which included tips on making bombs and suggested watching spy movies to learn tactics.

According to the FBI, there are ISIS terrorist investigations in all 50 states. However, these do seem to mostly be instance of lone wolves acting without foreign aid. Unlike France and Belgium—countries that have seen their citizens leave to be trained by ISIS in Syria only to return home to carry out terrorist attacks—America sees few militants actually trying to get back into the country. Therefore, the most dangerous threat to the United States is a "blended" attack—an attack inspired and directed by ISIS but carried out by a private citizen.

It is very difficult to determine how to prevent further domestic terrorism. The idea of banning Muslims from entering the country would do nothing to prevent current citizens from enlisting in ISIS remotely. The answer may be to promote the idea that ISIS's message is not an extremist Muslim utopia, as they claim, but a violent, brutal, and senseless pursuit. Many Muslims, such as Muhammad Jamal Khweis, are already spreading this idea. After deserting ISIS in 2015, he told Kurdish reporters, "My message to the American people is that life in Mosul [a city in Iraq] is really, really bad. The people who are controlling Mosul don't represent the religion. [Terrorist groups] don't represent the religion. I don't see them as good Muslims."[43] Having people testify to the horrors of ISIS before a national audience might convince those who have decided to join ISIS that their lives will be much worse if they do.

Future Battles

Terrorism has been around as long as governments have existed. It is often carried out in response to what governments represent. Terrorism is so frightening because it can happen anywhere, does not require much money or resources, and, when it happens, can cause a major loss of life. Terrorism is very different from conventional war. Wars come to an end because supplies deplete and a victory is determined. Terrorism can come from any small group of people who already accept that they might not see a victory.

CNN conducted a poll in 2016 that found that Americans think terrorist attacks are more likely now than at any time since 2003. After the September 11 attacks, Americans have been very concerned about plane hijacking by a terrorist organization. Since the San Bernardino shootings and the 2016 tragedy in Orlando, Americans have grown much more concerned about lone-wolf terrorism. Despite this fear, only a small percentage of the total deaths from terrorism actually took place in Western countries, and that percentage is even smaller when considering the number of deaths on American soil. Most deaths from terrorism happen in the Middle East, where ISIS holds power.

The question remains as to how the United States will fight future terrorism. Trump's staff has talked about reintroducing the torture of imprisoned terrorists and even killing the families of known terrorists. Some think valuable information could be obtained from torture because radical Muslims could be keeping secrets about terrorists in their own communities. Many disagree with this, including the CIA. One former FBI agent explained that other Western countries that see terrorist attacks, such as France and Germany, differ greatly from the United States. There is less of a sense of integrated community because European countries are close geographically but separated by country borders. In America, Muslims are much better integrated, and to accuse them of criminal activity with little proof "destroys any future cooperation, and it feeds directly to [the teachings] of radical terrorist groups—that the United States and the West are at war with Islam, at war with Muslims everywhere."[44] This is clearly harmful to attempts to stop the spread of terror.

Meanwhile, the DHS continues to work across the country and around the world to defend the United States against threats and attacks. It has implemented the Nationwide Suspicious Activity Reporting Initiative that trains "state and local law enforcement to recognize behaviors and indicators related to terrorism, crime and other threats while standardizing how those observations are documented and shared with FBI Joint Terrorism Task Forces (JTTFs) for investigation."[45] It has also implemented Secure Flight, which is a program requiring the TSA to screen every passenger flying either within the United States or across its borders against government terrorist watchlists.

There is no surefire way to prevent terrorism—only ways to attempt to. Unlike other crimes, the faces and methods of terrorism have changed countless times over the course of U.S. history. What the world recognizes as terrorism today will likely change drastically in 100 years. However, these changes give the United States—and the world—opportunities to learn how to better protect its land and citizens in an evolving world.

Notes

Introduction: What Is Terrorism?

1. Federal Bureau of Investigation, "Terrorism 2002/2005," U.S. Department of Justice, accessed May 31, 2017. www.fbi.gov/stats-services/publications/terrorism-2002-2005.

2. Quoted in Andrew Shaver, "You're More Likely to be Fatally Crushed by Furniture than Killed by a Terrorist," *Washington Post*, November 23, 2015. www.washingtonpost.com/news/monkey-cage/wp/2015/11/23/youre-more-likely-to-be-fatally-crushed-by-furniture-than-killed-by-a-terrorist/?utm_term=.553c9dfc4083.

Chapter One: Terrorism in 19th Century America

3. T. B. H. Stenhouse, *The Rocky Mountain Saints: A Full and Complete History of the Mormons, from the First Vision of Joseph Smith to the Last Courtship of Brigham Young*. New York, NY: D. Appleton and Company, 1873, p. 458.

4. Quoted in Will Bagley, *Blood of the Prophets: Brigham Young and the Massacre at Mountain Meadows*. Norman, OK: University of Oklahoma Press, 2002, p. 176.

5. Quoted in J. Michael Martinez, *Terrorist Attacks on American Soil: From the Civil War Era to the Present*. Plymouth, UK: Rowman & Littlefield, 2012, p. 60.

6. Quoted in Martinez, *Terrorist Attacks on American Soil*, p. 65.

7. Quoted in Randall Kennedy, *For Discrimination: Race, Affirmative Action, and the Law*. New York, NY: Vintage Books, 2013, p. 23.

Chapter Two: Terrorism in 20th Century America

8. Quoted in Beverly Gage, *The Day Wall Street Exploded: A Story of America in Its First Age of Terror*. New York, NY: Oxford University Press, 2009, p. 148.

9. Quoted in Randall D. Law, *Terrorism: A History*. Cambridge, UK: Polity Press, 2009, p. 124.

10. Martinez, *Terrorist Attacks on American Soil*, p. 178.

11. Quoted in Deborah George, ed., "'Segregation Forever': A Fiery Pledge Forgiven, But Not Forgotten," NPR, accessed June 1, 2017. www.npr.org/2013/01/14/169080969/segregation-forever-a-fiery-pledge-forgiven-but-not-forgotten.

12. Quoted in Martinez, *Terrorist Attacks on American Soil*, p. 222.

Chapter Three: Domestic Bombings

13. Quoted in Alston Chase, *A Mind for Murder: The Education of the Unabomber and the Origins of Modern Terrorism*. New York, NY: W.W. Norton & Co., 2003, p. 177.

14. Quoted in Chase, *A Mind for Murder*, p. 18.

15. Quoted in Martinez, *Terrorist Attacks on American Soil*, p. 247.

16. Quoted in Martinez, *Terrorist Attacks on American Soil*, p. 250.

17. Quoted in Chase, *A Mind for Murder*, p. 76.

18. Quoted in Chase, *A Mind for Murder*, p. 84.

19. Quoted in Alston Chase, "Harvard and the Making of the Unabomber," *The Atlantic*, June 2000. www.theatlantic.com/magazine/archive/2000/06/harvard-and-the-making-of-the-unabomber/378239/.

20. Quoted in Chase, *A Mind for Murder*, p. 79.

21. Quoted in Lou Michel and Dan Herbeck, *American Terrorist: Timothy McVeigh and the Oklahoma City Bombing*. New York, NY: HarperCollins, 2002. PDF e-book.

22. Quoted in Martinez, *Terrorist Attacks on American Soil*, p. 305.

23. Quoted in Martinez, *Terrorist Attacks on American Soil*, p. 321.

24. Thomas B. Edsall, "Clinic Bombing Probed for Link to Rudolph," *New York Times*, Mary 14, 1999. www.washingtonpost.com/archive/politics/1999/03/14/clinic-bombing-probed-for-link-to-rudolph/6c369eb1-abcf-451b-a872-3b4b92be4de2/?utm_term=.e2e236d57a07.

25. Eric Rudolph, "Full Text of Eric Rudolph's Confession," NPR, April 14, 2005. www.npr.org/templates/story/story.php?storyId=4600480.

26. Rudolph, "Full Text of Eric Rudolph's Confession."

Chapter Four: Al-Qaeda and the World Trade Center Attacks

27. Quoted in David L. Hudson, *The Handy American History Answer Book*. Canton, MI: Visible Ink Press, 2015. PDF e-book.

28. Quoted in Peg Tyre, "'Proud terrorist' gets life for Trade Center bombing," CNN, January 8, 1998. www.cnn.com/US/9801/08/yousef.update/.

29. National Commission on Terrorist Attacks upon the United States, *The 9/11 Commission Report: Final Report of the National Commission*

on *Terrorist Attacks upon the United States*. Washington, D.C.: U.S. Government Printing Office, 2004, p. 72.

30. Quoted in J. Michael Martinez, *The Safety of the Kingdom: Government Responses to Subversive Threats*. New York, NY: Carrel, 2015. PDF e-book.

31. Quoted in Martinez, *Terrorist Attacks on American Soil*, p. 370.

32. National Commission on Terrorist Attacks upon the United States, *The 9/11 Commission Report*, p. 11.

33. Department of Homeland Security, "Creation of the Department of Homeland Security," Department of Homeland Security, September 24, 2015. www.dhs.gov/creation-department-homeland-security.

Chapter Five: Terrorism After September 11

34. Quoted in Chelsea J. Carter, "Nidal Hasan Convicted in Fort Hood Shootings; Jurors can Decide Death," CNN, August 23, 2013. www.cnn.com/2013/08/23/justice/nidal-hasan-court-martial-friday/.

35. Quoted in Josh Rubin and Marr Smith, "'I am the Shooter,' Nidal Hasan Tells Ford Hood Court-Martial," CNN, August 6, 2013. www.cnn.com/2013/08/06/justice/hasan-court-martial/.

36. Quoted in Yasmin Khorram, "Chattanooga Shooter Changed after Mideast Visit, Friend Says," CNN, September 15, 2015. www.cnn.com/2015/07/17/us/tennessee-shooter-mohammad-youssuf-abdulazeez/.

37. Quoted in Khorram, "Chattanooga Shooter Changed after Mideast Visit, Friend Says."

38. Quoted in Kristina Sgueglia, "Chattanooga Shootings 'Inspired' by Terrorists, FBI Chief Says," CNN, December 16, 2015. www.cnn.com/2015/12/16/us/chattanooga-shooting-terrorist-inspiration/index.html.

39. Barack Obama, "Address to the Nation by the President," White House, December 6, 2015. obamawhitehouse.archives.gov/the-press-office/2015/12/06/address-nation-president.

Chapter Six: Battling Terrorism Today

40. Quoted in Sumit Galhotra, "Domestic Terror: Are we Doing Enough to Combat the Threat From Within?," CNN, September 17, 2012. www.cnn.com/2012/09/16/us/domestic-terrorism/index.html.

41. "Secretary of Homeland Security," Department of Homeland Security, January 25, 2017. www.dhs.gov/secretary.

42. Harry Truman, "National Security Council Intelligence Directive No. 9 Revised," in "Foreign Relations of the United States 1950–1955, The Intelligence Community, 1950–1955," Douglas Keane, Michael Warner, and Edward C. Keefer, eds. Washington, D.C.: U.S. Government Printing Office, 2007. HTML e-book.

43. Quoted in Rebecca Kheel, "American ISIS Fighter: 'I Wasn't Thinking Straight,'" The Hill, March 18, 2016. thehill.com/policy/defense/273541-american-isis-fighter-i-wasnt-thinking-straight.

44. Quoted in Siddhartha Mahanta, "Fighting Terrorism in the Age of Trump," *The Atlantic*, November 12, 2017. www.theatlantic.com/international/archive/2016/11/trump-torture-soufan-fbi-al-qaeda-isis-islam/507380/.

45. "DHS' Progress in 2011: Enhancing Partnerships with State and Local Law Enforcement," Department of Homeland Security, July 29, 2016. www.dhs.gov/dhs-progress-2011-enhancing-partnerships-state-and-local-law-enforcement.

For More Information

Books

Dwyer, Jim, and Kevin Flynn. *102 Minutes: The Unforgettable Story of the Fight to Survive Inside the Twin Towers*. New York, NY: Times Books, 2005. This powerful book describes the scene inside the World Trade Center after the September 11 attacks.

Freeman, Jim. *UNABOMBER: How the FBI Broke Its Own Rules to Capture the Terrorist Ted Kaczynski*. Palisades, NY: History Publishing Company, 2014. This book tells the story of how the FBI had to become friendly with the media to catch the Unabomber, signaling a significant shift in the way the agency worked.

Morell, Michael. *The Great War of Our Time: The CIA's Fight Against Terrorism—From al Qa'ida to ISIS*. New York, NY: Hachette Book Group, 2015. Michael Morell worked for the CIA at the time of the September 11 attacks—his book is an insight into the CIA's counterterrorism successes and failures in fighting against extremist Muslims.

Sageman, Marc. *Misunderstanding Terrorism*. Philadelphia, PA: University of Pennsylvania Press, 2017. This book offers the controversial view that groups such as ISIS are only strengthened by America's counterterrorism actions.

Weimann, Gabriel. *Terrorism in Cyberspace*. New York, NY: Columbia University Press, 2015. This book explains how terrorists and organizations can use the Internet to create as much chaos as a bomb blast.

Websites

Department of Homeland Security (www.dhs.gov)
This is the official website of the Department of Homeland Security; it has links to detailed reports of its counterterrorist actions.

Global Terrorism Database (www.start.umd.edu/gtd/)
Hosted by the University of Maryland, this detailed site gives users access to thousands of articles and data points about terrorism across the world.

National Counterterroism Center (www.nctc.gov)
The National Counterterrorism Center is one of the most powerful tools the United States has for fighting extremism across the globe, and this website details that organization.

"The Rising Homegrown Terror Threat on the Right" (theconversation.com/the-rising-homegrown-terror-threat-on-the-right-78242)
This well-researched article gives details on one of America's most troubling emerging problems: right-wing political terrorism.

United Nations Actions to Counter Terrorism (www.un.org/en/counterterrorism/)
The United Nations is unified in its fight against global terror organizations, and its website explains what actions it has taken and how effective they have been.

Index

A
Abdel-Rahman, Omar, 60
Abdulazeez, Mohammad Youssuf, 7, 76–78
abortion, 53, 55
Abouhalima, Mahoud, 58, 60
Afghanistan, 9, 56, 58, 63, 71, 76, 82
Ajaj, Ahmed, 58, 60
Alfred P. Murrah Federal Building, 43, 47, 49
American Airlines Flight 77, 64
American Anarchist Fighters, 27
American Civil War, 15, 17–18, 23, 33, 90
American Revolution, 12
America's Most Wanted (TV show), 55
Army of God, 54
assisted suicide, 48
Atta, Mohammed, 63–64
Ayers, Bill, 35
Ayyad, Nidal, 58, 60

B
al-Baghdadi, Abu Bakr, 7, 83–84
Baker-Fancher party, 14–15
Baxley, Bill, 32
Birmingham, Alabama, 6, 29, 32, 54
Blackburn, Luke Pryor, 15–18
Border and Transportation Security, 67
Boston Marathon, 7, 73–74
Boston Tea Party, 12
Branch Davidian raid, 46–48, 54
Branham, Thomas, 53
Buchanan, James, 14
Burns, William J., 24, 26
Bush, George W., 7

C
California Forestry Association, 42
Carlin, John, 90
Carter, Jimmy, 86
Catholics, 33
Centennial Olympic Park, 51–53
Central Intelligence Agency (CIA), 6, 62–63, 81, 86–88, 92
Chambliss, Robert, 32
Chemical, Biological, Radiological and Nuclear Countermeasures, 67
Civil Rights Act, 18
civil rights movement, 29–30, 32–33
Clinton, Bill, 47
Coast Guard, 86
Colfax Massacre, 6, 18, 20, 22
Comey, James, 76–77
Confederate soldiers, 33
Congress, 18, 86, 88
Constitution, 18
countercultural movement, 33
Counterterrorism Center (CTC), 6, 62–63, 67
Counterterrorist Intelligence Centers, 62
Crist, Buckley, Jr., 38–39
Customs and Border Protection, 86
cyberwarfare, 88

D
Darrow, Clarence, 25
Davis, Tom, 51
Declaration of Jihad on the Americans Occupying the Country of the Two Holiest Sites, 7, 62
Department of Defense, 88
Department of Homeland Security (DHS), 67–68, 70, 85–86, 90, 92

Dr. Black Vomit, 15, 17

E
Emergency Preparedness and Response, 67
Enforcement Act, 22

F
Facebook, 78
Farook, Syed Rizwan, 7, 78–79
Farouq mosque, 60
Federal Emergency Management Agency (FEMA), 86
Fort Hood, 7, 71, 78
Fortier, Michael, 46, 48, 50
14th Amendment, 18
Freedom Club (FC), 40
Freedmen's Bureau, 18

G
Goldman, Emma, 28
Grant, Ulysses S., 18

H
Hanson, Peter, 64
Harvard University, 38
Hasan, Nidal Malik, 7, 71–73
al-Hazmi, Nawaf, 64
Henry A. Murray Research Center, 38
Holocaust, 53
Hoover, J. Edgar, 27, 31–32
Hughes, Jermaine Jerome, 54
Hussein, Saddam, 62
Hyams, Godfrey, 17

I
Immigration Services, 86
Industrial Revolution, 45
Information Analysis and Infrastructure Protection, 67
International Association of Bridge and Structural Workers, 23

Iran, 90
Iraq, 9, 51, 76, 81–83, 85, 90–91
Iraq War, 71
Islamic State of Iraq and Syria (ISIS), 7–8, 11, 78–79, 81–85, 90–91
Islamophobia, 10, 85, 90
Ismoil, Eyad, 60

J
Japanese Red Army, 62
Jarrah, Ziad, 64
Jewell, Richard, 51, 53
Jews, 33, 62
jihad, 7, 58, 62, 71, 76
Johnson, Andrew, 17–19
Joint Terrorism Task Forces (JTTFs), 92

K
Kaczynski, Ted, 6, 36–40, 42–45, 85, 88, 90
Kahneman, Daniel, 10
Kennedy, John F., 31, 36
Khweis, Muhammad Jamal, 91
King, Martin Luther, Jr., 29–30
Koresh, David, 48
Ku Klux Klan (KKK), 6, 22, 29, 33, 46

L
Bin Laden Issue Station, 62
bin Laden, Osama, 6–7, 27, 56–58, 60, 62–64, 67–69, 72, 78, 82–83, 88, 90
Lee, John D., 15
Libya, 90
Lincoln, Abraham, 15, 17–18
lone-wolf terrorism, 71, 79, 82, 85, 91
Lopez, Ivan, 7, 71, 73
Los Angeles Times, 23–25

M
Malik, Tashfeen, 7, 78–79
Massachusetts Institute of Technology, 73

Mateen, Omar, 7, 79–81
McManigal, Ortie, 25
McNamara, John J., 25
McVeigh, Timothy, 7, 43–48, 50–51, 85, 88
al-Mihdhar, Khalid, 64
Mohammed, Khalid Shaikh, 60
Mormons, 12, 14–15, 18
Mosser, Thomas, 40
Mountain Meadows Massacre, 12–13, 88
mujahideen, 58
Murray, Gilbert, 42
Murtagh, John M., 34
Muslims, 6, 10–11, 27, 56, 58, 62–63, 68, 71–73, 76, 78, 82–83, 85, 90–92

N
Nash, Christopher Columbus, 21–22
National Clandestine Service, 6, 62
National Security Agency (NSA), 6, 63, 88
Nationwide Suspicious Activity Reporting Initiative, 92
New York Stock Exchange, 25
New York Times, 40, 42–43
Nichols, Terry, 46–48, 50–51
9/11 Commission Report, 61
Northern Ireland Troubles, 9

O
Obama, Barack, 35, 69, 78–79
Office of Strategic Services, 86
Offices of the Naval and Army Intelligences, 86
Olympics, 51, 53–56
Orlando, Florida, 7, 9, 79–82, 91
Otis, Harrison Gray, 23–24

P
Paiute, 14
patriot movement, 51

Pearl Harbor, 88
Pentagon, 7, 35, 60, 64, 66
Pew Research Center, 70
post–traumatic stress disorder (PTSD), 46, 73
Princeton University, 10
psychologists, 42

Q
al-Qaeda, 10–11, 56, 58, 62–64, 67, 71, 79, 82–83, 85

R
Rudolph, Eric Robert, 51–56

S
Salameh, Mohammad, 58, 60
San Bernardino, California, 7, 78–79, 82, 91
schizophrenia, 42
Secret Service, 86
Secure Flight, 92
September 11th Victim Compensation Fund, 66
September 11, 2001, 8–10, 12, 43, 59, 62–68, 70–71, 79, 86, 90–91
16th Street Baptist Church bombing, 6, 29, 32–33
Smith, Joseph, 14
Snowden, Edward, 88–89
Somalia, 90
Southern Poverty Law Center, 51
Soviet Union, 58
Sudan, 90
surveillance, 35, 63, 70–71, 88
Syria, 7–9, 76, 78, 81–83, 85, 90–91

T
Transportation Security Administration (TSA), 86, 92
Truman, Harry S., 31, 88
Trump, Donald J., 90–91

Tsarnaev, Dzhokhar, 73, 76
Tsarnaev, Tamerlan, 73

U

Unabomber, 6–7, 36, 38–43
United Airlines Flight 93, 64
United Klans of America, 29
University of California, Berkeley, 38–39
University of Michigan, 38, 40
USA PATRIOT Act, 70
USS *Cole*, 63
Utah War, 15

V

Vietnam War, 33–36

W

Waco, Texas, 46–47, 54
Waheeb, Abu, 81
Wahhibism, 56
Wallace, George, 29
Wall Street, 25–28
Ward, William, 21
Washington Post, 43
watchlist, 92
Weathermen, 33–35
Weather Underground, 33–36
White House, 65, 69
white supremacy, 22, 29, 32
World Islamic Front for Jihad Against Jews and Crusaders, 62
World Trade Center, 6–7, 56, 58, 60–62, 64–65, 70, 82

Y

Yasin, Abdul Rahman, 60
yellow fever, 15, 17
Yemen, 63, 90
Young, Brigham, 14–15
Yousef, Ramzi, 6, 60–62

Z

al-Zarqawi, Abu Musab, 83

Picture Credits

Cover, pp. 4–5 Paul Turner/Contributor/Hulton Archive/Getty Images; p. 6 (top) Bettman/Contributor/Bettmann/Getty Images; p. 6 (bottom left) PAUL J. RICHARDS/Staff/AFP/Getty Images; p. 6 (bottom middle) Ralf-Finn Hestoft/Contributor/Corbis Historical/Getty Images; p. 6 (bottom right) Bryan Thomas/Stringer/Getty Images News/Getty Images; p. 7 (top left) BOB DAEMMRICH/Staff/AFP/Getty Images; p. 7 (top right) Sipa via AP Images; p. 7 (bottom) Spencer Platt/Staff/Getty Images News/Getty Images; p. 13 Joanne Ciccarello/Contributor/Christian Science Monitor/Getty Images; p. 16 Art Collection 3/Alamy Stock Photo; pp. 19, 26, 28, 30, 31, 59, 65 Courtesy of the Library of Congress; pp. 20–21, 24 Everett Historical/Shutterstock.com; p. 32 AP Photo/Hal Yeager; p. 37 Scott Manchester/Contributor/Sygma/Getty Images; p. 40 Allan Tannenbaum/Contributor/The LIFE Images Collection/Getty Images; p. 43 Mug Shot/Alamy Stock Photo; p. 46 Getty Images/Staff/Getty Images News/Getty Images; p. 49 AP Photo/David Longstreath; p. 52 Erik S. Lesser/Stringer/Getty Images News/Getty Images; p.57 MIR HAMID/DAILY DAWN/Contributor/Gamma-Rapho/Getty Images; p. 61 MARK D. PHILLIPS/Staff/AFP/Getty Images; p. 66 The Washington Post/Contributor/The Wahington Post/Getty Images; p. 68 Alex Wong/Staff/Getty Images News/Getty Images; pp. 72, 73 Handout/Handout/Getty Images News/Getty Images; pp. 74–75 Boston Globe/Contributor/Boston Globe/Getty Images; p. 77 Brent Lewis/Contributor/Denver Post/Getty Images; p. 79 U.S. Customs and Border Protection via AP, File; p. 80 Orlando Sentinel/Contributor/Tribune News Service/Getty Images; p. 83 AP Photo/Jacquelyn Martin; p. 84 Anadolu Agency/Contributor/Anadolu Agency/Getty Images; p. 87 SAUL LOEB/Staff/AFP/Getty Images; p. 89 Barton Gellman/Contributor/Getty Images News/Getty Images.

About the Author

Caroline Kennon is a college librarian originally from Yonkers, New York. She got her bachelor's and master's degrees in English from St. Bonaventure University in Western New York, and her master's degree in Library Science from the University at Buffalo. She is an avid reader, a novice cyclist, and a cheese addict. She currently lives in South Buffalo, New York—the winters really aren't that bad.